The Retirement Income Equation

Proven Strategies For Secure, Flexible, and Prosperous Retirement

Jeff Kikel ChFC, CRPC, CCFA

CPTX Media LLC

Published by CPTX Media, LLC, Cedar Park, Texas 78613

The publication is designed to provide accurate and authoritative information with regard to the subject matter covered. It is sold with the understanding that the publisher is not engaged in rendering financial, accounting, or other professional advice. If financial advice or other expertise is required, the services of a competent professional should be sought.

Contents

Dedication

I want to dedicate this book to Keith Kruk and Joe Veltri. Their mentorship and friendship helped me to bring this strategy to you.

Forward

As a member of Generation X, I often marvel at how quickly time flies. The months and years seem to slip through our fingers faster than ever, and with each passing day, the prospect of retirement looms larger. If you're like me, you may have set lofty goals for your retirement—dreaming of financial freedom and the opportunity to finally hang up your gloves and enjoy the fruits of your labor. I aimed to "retire" by age 55. While I achieved financial freedom at that milestone, I soon realized I wasn't prepared for retirement.

Retirement today looks vastly different from that of our parents and grandparents. Unlike them, most of us don't have the safety net of pensions. Instead, we've had to shoulder the responsibility of saving for retirement. This shift has brought both opportunities and uncertainties. We are navigating uncharted waters, and the stakes are high. I understand the challenges you're facing, and I'm here to help.

This realization led me to write "The Retirement Income Equation." My mission has evolved from working with a small group of clients to helping an entire generation understand the critical importance of retirement planning. Our generation, born between 1955 and 1968, is unique. We are on the cusp of retirement, yet the landscape has changed drastically, demanding a new approach to ensure security, flexibility, and prosperity in our golden years. Our generation is at the forefront of this change, and your role is crucial.

Early in my career, I learned the strategies that would evolve into the **Sure Horizon Retirement Income Strategy™**, which has become the cornerstone of my approach to retirement planning. This plan is built around three core goals: Guarantees, Flexibility, and Growth. These goals are achieved through three distinct elements: the Essential Pool, the Discretionary Pool, and the Growth Pool.

1. **The Essential Pool** ensures that guaranteed income sources like Social Security, pensions, and annuities cover your basic living expenses.

2. **The Discretionary Pool** provides the flexibility to enjoy retirement through activities and lifestyle choices that may vary over time. These could include travel, hobbies, or unexpected expenses like home repairs.

3. **The Growth Pool** is designed to ensure your assets continue to grow, combat inflation, and support your long-term financial needs.

This book is more than just a guide; it's a call to action. It's a practical roadmap to help you navigate the complexities of retirement planning, tailored specifically for those of us in the Later Baby Boom and Early Gen X. It's about taking control of your financial future, creating a plan that adapts to your life, and ensuring you have the security, flexibility, and growth necessary for a prosperous retirement. With this book, you can feel confident that you're prepared for the journey ahead.

I invite you to join me on this journey. With knowledge and a solid strategy, let's face the uncertainties of retirement planning head-on. This book will inspire and empower you to take action and build a retirement plan that meets your needs and exceeds your expectations.

Your future is in your hands. Let's make it a future filled with confidence, comfort, and the freedom to enjoy life fully. Together, we can ensure that your retirement is everything you've dreamed of and more. I urge you to take the first step today by diving into the pages of this book and starting your journey toward a prosperous retirement.

Welcome to "The Retirement Income Equation."

Jeff Kikel

Chapter 1

Introduction

Unlocking Your Retirement Potential

"Retirement is a journey, and your strategy is the map that guides you."

Imagine you're nearing retirement and just received a notification about your last paycheck. It hits you—this isn't just a regular pause; this is the threshold to a new era of your life. Suddenly, questions flood your mind. Will my savings last? What about medical emergencies? Can I maintain my lifestyle? Each question feels like a step into the unknown.

This chapter, indeed this book, begins with you and these questions. Over my three decades of helping people navigate retirement, I've seen the relief that dawns when a solid plan is in place. It's like watching someone find a map in a forest. That's what I aim to provide you—a map to your retirement, filled with clear paths and safe passages.

Retirement planning has shifted dramatically. It used to be that you worked till 65, got a gold watch, and lived off your pension and Social Security under a relatively predictable financial umbrella. Not anymore. Today, increasing life expectancies and the dynamic nature of the economy demand more than just saving; they require strategic planning.

This book is about understanding that retirement is no longer a brief period of winding down but a significant phase of life that could last as long as or longer than your working years. Here, you'll learn to survive and thrive in these golden years.

Let's paint a picture here. Without a robust retirement plan, you might face dwindling savings, with inflation chipping away at your buying power each year. Imagine hesitating to spoil your grandkids during the holidays or choosing between a utility bill and a medical prescription. It's not just about numbers and accounts—about the quality of your life, independence, and dignity.

The Promise Of This Book

This book culminates over 30 years of working with clients, preparing for and living in retirement. It shares my expertise learned over that time and the strategies I was taught early in my career.

I aim to share the disciplines of Financial and Retirement Planning, Insurance and Risk Management, and Investment Strategies as part of a holistic plan designed to help you successfully reach and live in retirement.

This book will help you learn more about building a successful retirement. You can do this yourself, but don't hesitate to contact me and my team if you would like some help.

Chapter 2
The New Retirement Reality

"Retirement is not about stepping back; it's about stepping into a new life with purpose and confidence."

Imagine you're a traveler setting out on a journey everyone must undertake—the retirement journey. Now, imagine how much the landscape for this journey has changed over the last few decades. It's almost as if the maps our parents or grandparents once used are entirely from another world. Today, the terrain of retirement planning is dramatically different, influenced by profound shifts in economic policies, societal norms, and technological advances.

Once upon a time, the path to retirement was well-marked and supported by sturdy, predictable structures—employer-sponsored pension plans. These plans promised a defined payout upon retirement, a reward for years of service that provided a transparent, direct route to financial security in one's later years. But as you look at the map now, you'll see that many of those paths have eroded, replaced by new routes that require more personal navigation than ever before. In most cases, these plans no longer exist, and for many of us, we don't just work for one company for our entire lives; we work at many.

Changing Landscapes

The shift from traditional pension plans to 401(k) plans and Individual Retirement Accounts (I.R.A.s) marks one of the most significant changes in the retirement planning landscape. Starting in 1974 with the passage of the Employee Retirement Income Security Act (E.R.I.S.A.), created to protect employees' retirements by establishing some minimum standards for retirement and healthcare plans, it significantly shifted who was responsible for employee retirement. This transformation reflects a broader move from defined benefit plans (pensions), where the retirement outcome was relatively certain, to defined contribution plans (401ks), where the result is uncertain and largely dependent on individual choices (and funding) and market performance.

This change has transferred the responsibility for retirement planning from the employer to the employee. Now, it's up to you to decide how much to save, where to invest, and how to manage those investments over time. While this shift offers more control and the potential for higher returns, it also introduces more risk. It requires a greater level of financial knowledge and active management.

Before I got into the financial services industry and started working in advertising, I didn't know what a 401k was or what the mutual funds I was investing in. My boss told me I should invest in my future, and I followed her advice (thank you, Julie McClure), and ignorance was bliss. Beyond that, I did not seek out any other advice and had no guidance. I was wandering in the woods with no map or compass, much like many of you have done up to this point. It was when I became a Registered Financial Advisor that I really gained an understanding of the importance of planning. Not everybody gets that opportunity.

Many of you out there are experts in your field and want to avoid taking on a second career as a finance professional. Whether you want to or not, you need to better understand the process. That is the reason for this book, to give you the experience I have gained over all these years.

Economic Fluctuations

Economic fluctuations that can dramatically affect savings and investment strategies add to the complexity of modern retirement planning. Interest rates, for example, play a crucial role in determining retirement savings growth. In periods of low-interest rates (such as from 2008 to 2021), traditional savings and fixed-income investments yield less, pushing retirees and those nearing retirement to seek higher returns through riskier investments. For some, this scares the bejesus out of you. You are risk-averse, and investing in things like stocks and real estate makes you wake up in the middle of the night.

Market volatility further complicates the landscape. Financial markets can swing wildly due to factors ranging from political unrest to global pandemics, impacting the value of retirement portfolios and, by extension, the financial security of retirees. These fluctuations underscore the need for strategic, dynamic planning that adapts to changing economic conditions.

Increased Longevity

One of the most significant changes in the retirement landscape is the increase in longevity. Advances in healthcare mean that people are living longer, healthier lives, extending the retirement period that needs to be funded. This longevity is a double-edged sword; while it offers the wonderful prospect of more years to enjoy retirement, it also imposes the challenge of ensuring that retirement funds last as long as needed.

The need for longer-term strategies has never been more critical. Planning for a retirement that could span 30 years or more requires more savings and innovative, adaptive strategies considering longer-term market trends, healthcare advancements, and lifestyle changes.

Challenges and Opportunities

One of the most pervasive fears among those approaching retirement is not having enough saved to support their desired lifestyle. This concern is compounded by several factors, each influencing the ability to accumulate sufficient retirement funds. Many of you find yourself starting to save seriously only in the later stages of your career, missing out on the exponential growth that compound interest could have provided if started earlier. Up to this point, you have poured a ton of money into your kids, and Nike, Xbox, and education have been competing for your limited funds. Additionally, not knowing what percentage of income you need to set aside or budget constraints may have caused you to underestimate your future needs, further complicating the picture.

The challenge of accurately estimating how much you'll need for retirement must be balanced. Forecasting future living costs, potential medical expenses, and the impact of inflation is daunting for even the financially savvy. To navigate these waters, it's crucial to use detailed retirement calculators, seek professional financial advice, and regularly update retirement goals as circumstances change.

Managing Investment Risk

As the burden of retirement planning shifts increasingly to you, managing investment risks becomes critical. The cornerstone of risk management in any investment portfolio is diversification—spreading your investments across various asset classes, industries, geographical regions, and investment vehicles to mitigate the impact of poor performance in any single area.

Understanding one's risk tolerance is also vital. It dictates the composition of an investment portfolio and can change with age, financial situation, and nearing retirement. Strategies such as gradually shifting from stocks to more bonds or other fixed-income investments as one approaches retirement can help manage risk and stabilize the value of investment portfolios against market volatility.

Planning For An Uncertain Future

The future is inherently uncertain, and retirement planning must account for this uncertainty. Key among these uncertainties is healthcare needs, which can become a significant expense as one ages. Planning for these costs involves:

- Considering health insurance options.

- Potential long-term care insurance.

- Saving in health-specific accounts like Health Savings Accounts (H.S.A.s) if available.

Another significant uncertainty is the viability of Social Security benefits. With ongoing debates about the sustainability of the Social Security system, relying solely on these benefits for retirement income is risky. It's advisable to view Social Security as a supplement to other retirement income sources (which is what it was designed to be) rather than the foundation.

Opportunities For Proactive Planning

While these challenges may seem daunting, proactively approaching retirement planning turns these potential obstacles into opportunities. By starting early, saving aggressively, and investing wisely, you can meet and exceed your retirement income needs.

Proactive (and Holistic) planning empowers you to take control of your financial future, potentially achieving financial freedom and a comfortable retirement earlier than anticipated. It encourages a dynamic approach to managing retirement funds, regularly reviewing and adjusting plans as needed, and staying informed about financial management strategies and economic conditions.

Reflect On Where You Come From.

As we navigate the terrain of retirement planning, it's essential to pause and assess where you currently stand. Think of it as taking a moment to check your map and compass while hiking. This reflection helps you appreciate the ground covered and highlights the areas where you need to focus more energy. So, let's ask:

- **What steps have you already taken towards retirement planning?** You may have started saving a portion of your income, invested in a 401(k) or I.R.A., or purchased property as an investment. Acknowledge these steps, no matter how small, as each contributes to your journey.

- **Where do you feel you need to improve? Are aspects of your financial planning making you feel uneasy or underprepared?** Identifying these gaps is the first step in fortifying your retirement strategy. You may have neglected to consider healthcare costs, or perhaps your investments are not as diversified as they could be.

Taking stock of your current situation will help set the stage for the proactive measures you can take to enhance your financial security as you move closer to retirement.

Aspirations And Fears

Retirement planning is not just about numbers and strategies; it's deeply personal and often driven by our hopes and fears. Understanding these emotional elements can provide powerful motivation and effectively direct your planning efforts. Consider the following:

- **What are your biggest hopes regarding your retirement?** Are you looking forward to traveling the world, spending more time with family, or perhaps indulging in hobbies you've never had time for? These aspirations should guide your financial planning, ensuring you can afford these dreams.

- **What are your biggest fears?** Many fear outliving their savings or facing significant health issues without adequate financial support. Recognizing these fears allows you to address them directly through your financial planning. For example, saving more aggressively or investing in long-term care insurance could mitigate these concerns.

How can understanding your current financial landscape help address these hopes and fears? Mapping your current financial situation gives you a baseline from which to build. It allows you to identify the most effective steps to secure the retirement you aspire to while safeguarding against the fears that could undermine your peace of mind.

Chapter Exercises

Exercise 1: Map Your Current Financial Landscape

Purpose: This exercise is designed to give you a comprehensive view of your current financial status regarding your retirement planning. By assessing your savings, income sources, and projected needs, you can identify potential gaps and areas that require more attention.

Steps:

1. **List Current Savings:** List all your current retirement savings accounts (e.g., 401(k), I.R.A., pensions, other savings). Note the total current balances.

2. **Identify Income Sources:** Note any current and future predictable income

sources you will have during retirement. This could include Social Security, annuities, rental incomes, or part-time work.

3. **Project Healthcare Costs:** Research and estimate your potential healthcare costs in retirement. Consider factors such as Medicare coverage, supplemental insurance, and out-of-pocket expenses.

4. **Calculate Lifespan:** Use an online life expectancy calculator to estimate how long your retirement savings need to last. Consider family health history and lifestyle factors.

Outcome: Completing this exercise will help you visualize your financial landscape clearly, identifying where you are well-prepared and where you might need to increase your efforts.

Looking Ahead: What's Next?

The next chapter will explore the new retirement realities and how they affect you. We'll explore the shift from traditional pension plans to more individual-centric retirement planning like 401(k)s and I.R.A.s. We'll also tackle the economic fluctuations that can impact your retirement savings and strategies and discuss the implications of increased longevity on your planning.

Furthermore, we will outline actionable strategies to address these challenges, turning potential obstacles into opportunities for a robust and secure retirement. You'll learn how to effectively manage investment risks, plan for uncertainties, and, most importantly, how proactive planning can transform these challenges into a solid foundation for your retirement.

Join me in the next chapter as we build on the groundwork we've laid today, ensuring that every step you take brings you closer to the retirement you envision and deserve.

Chapter 3

Your Retirement Your Terms

"The most successful retirements are built on a foundation of knowledge, strategy, and adaptability."

Welcome to a chapter that is all about empowerment—your empowerment. Retirement is not a one-size-fits-all journey, and this chapter is dedicated to helping you define what success in retirement looks like for you. Gone are the days when retirement meant stepping back and slowing down. Today, retirement is about stepping into a new phase of life on your terms, with the freedom to pursue what matters most to you.

In this era, you have more control over your retirement outcomes. This chapter will explore how you can harness that control to craft a retirement that fits your unique vision and needs. Whether you dream of globe-trotting adventures, pursuing passions, or simply enjoying a quiet and comfortable life surrounded by loved ones, it's all about making those dreams practical.

Setting The Stage For Strategic Planning

Retirement planning today requires more than just understanding finances; it requires understanding yourself. What do you want your days to look like when you no longer have to work? How do you want to manage your time, energy, and resources? These are deeply personal questions; the answers will guide constructing a retirement plan that genuinely serves you.

This chapter will provide the tools to visualize your ideal retirement, set clear goals, and create a flexible plan that adapts to life's changes. We'll cover how to:

- Envision your perfect retirement lifestyle.

- Understand the financial implications of your choices.

- Strategically plan to make your vision a reality.

Tailoring Strategies To Fit Your Life

Every retirement plan should be different because no two lives are exactly alike. That does not mean that we eliminate structure. As we delve into the nuances of creating a retirement plan that reflects your aspirations and circumstances, you'll learn how to adjust standard financial advice to better suit your situation. This chapter will encourage you to think about what you want from retirement and empower you with the strategies to achieve it.

Stay tuned as we embark on this journey of discovery and planning. By the end of this chapter, you'll have a clearer picture of how to build your retirement on your terms, ensuring that it's not just a time of life but a time of living well.

The Power of Preparedness

Transforming Uncertainties Into Opportunities

Preparedness in retirement planning doesn't just safeguard your finances; it transforms potential stressors into opportunities for personal growth and enjoyment. This principle is vividly illustrated through the experiences of individuals like Maria and Jack below, who turned their retirement uncertainties into well-earned successes.

Highlighting the Benefits

The benefits of being prepared extend beyond the tangible outcomes of financial strategies. They imbue retirees with a sense of control and confidence that is invaluable. Here are the key benefits of a well-prepared retirement plan:

- **Financial Security:** The most obvious benefit is financial security. Knowing that your finances are well-organized and that you have strategies to handle fluctuations gives you a solid foundation for enjoying your retirement years.

- **Peace of Mind:** There's a deep comfort in knowing you are prepared for whatever may come. This peace of mind is priceless as it allows you to focus on enjoying life rather than worrying about what-if scenarios.

- **Freedom to Enjoy Retirement:** With the primary concerns addressed and planned, you can pursue the activities you love. Whether traveling, picking up new hobbies, or spending time with family, being prepared means these joys are not overshadowed by financial worries.

- **Adaptability to Changes:** Preparedness isn't about having a fixed path but a flexible strategy that can adapt to changes, whether personal, economic, or social. This adaptability is crucial in today's ever-changing world.

Client Scenario: Maria's Market Mastery

Maria started thinking seriously about retirement in her mid-40s. With a volatile market and economic uncertainties looming, she recognized the need for a strategic approach to her retirement savings. Working with a financial planner, Maria diversified her investment portfolio, balancing aggressive growth stocks and stable, income-generating bonds. This careful planning allowed her to remain calm and collected during economic downturns, viewing them as opportunities rather than setbacks.

When a significant market downturn occurred, instead of panicking, Maria saw an opportunity to buy additional stocks at a lower price, guided by her well-structured investment plan. This strategy paid off remarkably well in the long run, allowing her portfolio to grow significantly as the market recovered. Thanks to her foresight and proactive planning, Maria entered retirement with a robust portfolio and the confidence that she could manage her finances effectively under market conditions.

Jack's Health Horizon

Jack was acutely aware of his family history of health issues and knew managing healthcare costs would be crucial in his retirement planning. He enhanced his health insurance coverage and started a health savings account, setting aside funds for future medical expenses. Since Jack was limited in how much he could contribute each year, he chose to contribute to the HSA each year and pay for medical expenses out of pocket. He invested the funds in his HSA account in a growth portfolio. This proactive approach proved invaluable when Jack faced an unexpected health challenge shortly after retiring.

Thanks to his comprehensive insurance and the extra savings, Jack could afford top-tier medical treatment without the burden of financial stress. His preparation meant that instead of depleting other retirement savings, he could focus on recovery and enjoying his life post-treatment. Jack's foresight in planning for health expenses ensured his retirement was defined not by financial strain but by his recovery and continued enjoyment of life.

What We Can Learn

The stories of Maria and Jack underscore the profound benefits of being prepared:

- **Financial Security and Control:** Maria's experience shows that a well-planned investment strategy can turn market volatility into a growth opportunity, enhancing financial security.

- **Peace of Mind:** Jack's ability to handle unexpected health issues without financial distress highlights the peace of mind from targeted saving and insurance strategies.

- **Freedom to Enjoy Retirement:** Both examples illustrate that with major concerns addressed beforehand, retirees can freely pursue their passions and enjoy their leisure years without the cloud of financial worries.

- **Adaptability to Changes:** The flexibility in their plans allowed Maria and Jack to adapt to new circumstances, proving that a good retirement plan is sturdy and flexible.

These narratives demonstrate that thorough planning and readiness are not just about staving off potential disasters—they're about creating a framework within which retirees can thrive, no matter what challenges or opportunities arise.

Final Thoughts

This chapter gave you an idea of some of the things you need to consider as you build your Retirement Income Strategy. Whether it is income for essential expenses such as shelter, food, healthcare, or discretionary expenses such as travel, your plan must cover ALL these expenses.

The next chapter will cover several retirement income strategies used in the Financial Industry. I will also introduce you to an approach I have used with clients for almost 30 years, the Sure Horizon Retirement Income Strategy™.

Hold on tight. It gets fun from here as we build a plan for you.

Part I: Understanding The Essentials

Chapter 4

Retirement Income Strategies

"In retirement, guarantees are your financial foundation. Build them wisely."

R etirement planning can often seem complex and overwhelming, but it doesn't have to be. With the proper structure, you can ensure a steady flow of income that meets all your needs throughout retirement.

Before we get into strategies, we need to understand what a retirement income plan needs to include to be successful.

The first thing you need to understand is that there are three key elements that every Retirement Income Plan needs to include:

- **Guarantees:** This element covers essential expenses such as housing, food, and healthcare. These non-negotiable expenses must be met consistently, making reliable income sources like Social Security, pensions, and income annuities crucial.

- **Flexibility:** Managing discretionary expenses such as travel, hobbies, and entertainment. This plan aspect deals with varying expenses and offers more personal choice. The flexibility comes from having income sources that can be adjusted as needed, like bond ladders or other liquid investments.

- **Growth:** The final element ensures ongoing financial security against inflation and increasing costs over time. This involves investing in assets with the potential for appreciation and generating returns that outpace inflation, ensuring your purchasing power remains strong throughout retirement.

As we build your retirement income plan, we must ensure these elements are part of it. In addition to these three elements, there are three crucial financial goals that retirees must meet:

- **Essential Expense Goal:** This is the scary and most crucial goal for retirees and keeps people up at night. Essential expenses such as housing, food, and healthcare are non-negotiable and must be met consistently. Reliable income sources such as Social Security, Pensions, or Income Annuities are typically used to meet this goal.

- **Discretionary Expense Goal:** This aspect of the plan deals with expenses that can vary and offers more personal choices. I have always called this the "Fun Bucket." This is where travel, hobbies, and entertainment reside. Since these expenses can vary, this part of your plan must be flexible.

- **Long-Term Growth Goal:** The final element ensures ongoing financial security against inflation and increasing costs over time. This involves investing in assets with the potential for appreciation and generating returns that outpace inflation, ensuring your purchasing power remains strong throughout retirement.

Now that we understand the Three Elements of Retirement Plans and The Three Goals, we can look at some of the strategies used for retirement income planning.

Our Grandparents Approach

If you reading this book, you are likely a Late Baby Boomer (1955-65) or an Early Gen X'er (1965-1976). I am an Early Gen X'er (born in 1967), so many things we will discuss in the book are also on my mind. Most of us had grandparents whose formative years were during the Great Depression and World War 2. They experienced economic collapse, bank failures, and some of the most significant stock market drops early in their lives. As a result, this generation tended to be more conservative with their investments. They also lived through relatively high interest rates (unfortunately, not as high at the end of their lives).

The Greatest Generation, as they were called by Tom Brokaw (TV News Personality and Author), had pretty simple retirement plans. Most worked for companies for 30-40 years and retired with a pension, social security, and savings. That savings was typically invested in Long Term Bonds.

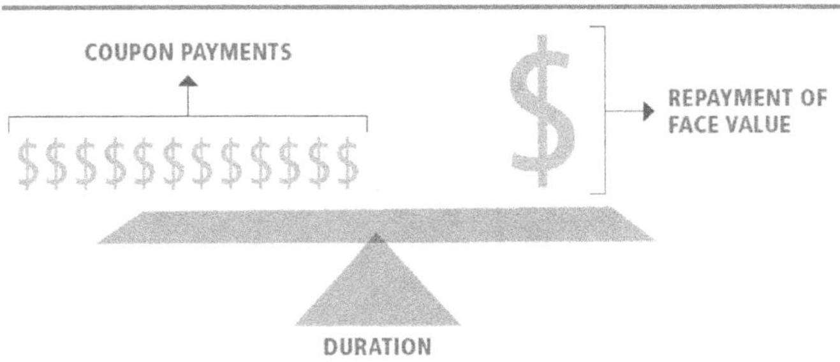

Image courtesy of Pimco Advisors

This strategy initially worked exceptionally well for this generation because many retired in the late 1970s and early 1980s. Inflation was extremely high, so US Treasury bonds were in the 17-18% range. As inflation dropped through the early 1980s, these bonds were locked in at higher rates. People using this strategy invest money and earn interest (either monthly, quarterly, or semi-annually). This strategy works well if interest rates remain high or inflation remains tame.

The first problem with this strategy is that as inflation rises, eventually, your interest does not keep up, and you can reach a point where you might need to liquidate some of your bonds to pay for expenses. This liquidation reduces your interest income over time.

The second problem with this strategy is if you retire during a period of low interest rates, such as was experienced by the Leading Edge Boomers (1945-1955) as they retired in the mid-2000s. It probably worked if you had a very large investment portfolio then. However, if you had a smaller portfolio, you might have needed more income to pay your bills. In the past couple of years, inflation has risen dramatically while interest rates have lagged, causing many retirees with more conservative portfolios to struggle.

Now that we understand the strategy, let's run it through the filter of the 3 elements that every retirement plan needs to have:

1. **Guarantees:** Depending on what bonds you choose to invest in, these are typically not guaranteed. However, US Treasury Bonds have some of the highest credit quality in the world, so we will give them the benefit of the doubt here.

2. **Flexibility:** Most bonds are reasonably liquid and can be sold; however, when sold, they reduce your income in the future. In addition, changes in interest rates will affect the price you get for your bonds. If rates are higher when you sell your bonds, you will typically take a loss on the price. You can sell your bonds at a higher price if rates are lower. Think of a teeter-totter: when bond yields are down, prices rise; bond prices drop when bond yields are higher.

3. **Growth:** Absolutely zilch if you hold the bonds to maturity. This can be a big problem as inflation always continues.

As you can see, the Bond Income Strategy popular with our Grandparents can be extremely risky over time as inflation and the economy change. Let's look at the other end of the spectrum, taking income from a diversified investment portfolio.

Diversified Investment Portfolio Income Strategy

Well, we tried the bond strategy, and while it feels pretty good in crazy times, we can see it in the world. It fell apart when we began to experience inflation, as we have seen since 2021.

What is another solution? We could diversify our assets into a portfolio of Stocks, Bonds, and Cash. This could be done through individual securities, mutual funds, or exchange-traded funds. You are probably familiar with this because it was how you built up your portfolio during the accumulation phase of your career, putting money in every paycheck into a 401k or saving into an IRA each year. Markets went up, and markets went down (we have seen some doozies in our lifetime), but we are true believers, and we knew as long as we held on, things would eventually come back. Plus, we could buy our investments on sale when things were down.

Fast-forward to retirement, and now we must start generating income from our diversified portfolio. No more money is coming in; now, just money is coming out. The theory behind this strategy is that you will withdraw 3-4% per year from your portfolio. Let's say we build a balanced portfolio (50% Stock/50% Bonds) that generates, on average, 5.5%. Your portfolio should support you for the rest of your life.

The one challenge is whether returns are really average. Nope.

Returns average over time; however, in any given year, the markets can wildly gyrate in either direction. That also assumes that you keep your asset allocation consistent (which we know doesn't happen) and don't sell out when things get bad and not get back in the market.

Let me give you a real-life example of what happened in my early career in the Financial Services Industry. In 2000, I worked for five years at one of the largest brokerage firms in the country and thought I knew everything there was to know about the markets. The world was wonderful after five years of a bull market and anything with a Dot Com attached to it going into the stratosphere.

One of my clients, whom we will call Rick, was an executive at a large communications company in Dallas, Texas, where I worked at the time. With the highs in the markets and the growth of his portfolio, Rick decided to go out on top and retire. During this time, interest rates were low, and with stocks at a high, clients wanted more exposure to stocks. The idea was that you could get a 10% (Average) return in the stock market, pull out 4-5% (the common thought at the time) in income, and continue to build your portfolio. That all works until it doesn't work.

In 2000, the Dot Com and Tech Bubble burst in March. Here is what the math looked like for Rick, who had most of his money in the "Safe" and "Diversified" S&P 500.

Figure 3.1

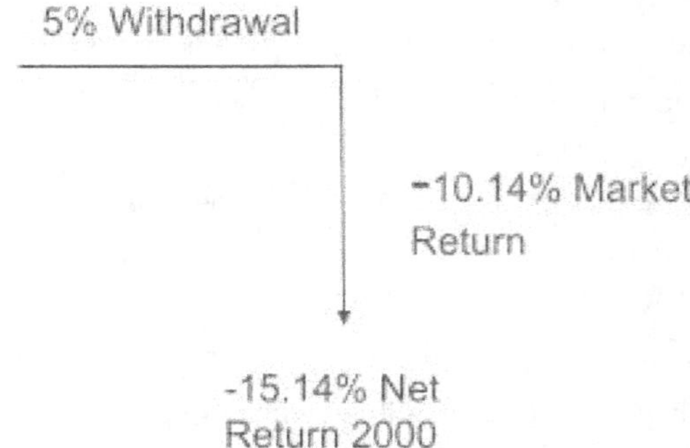

In 2000, the S&P 500 dropped **10.14%**, and as you can see in Figure 3.1, we also took out our 5% income for that year. Rick's portfolio was down **15.14%** at the end of the year. Rick was unhappy, but he knew the market would eventually return.

Figure 3.2

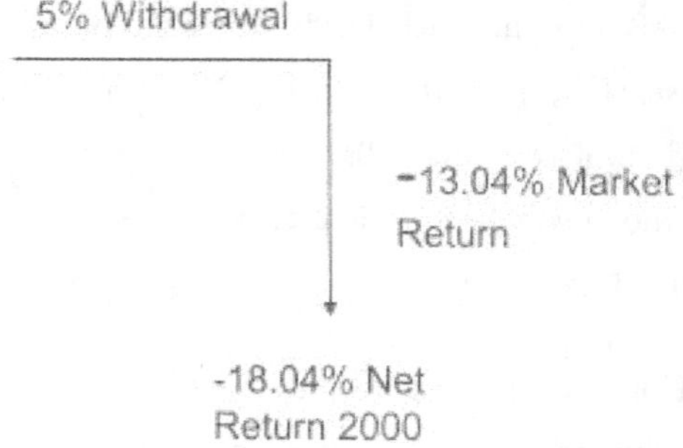

2001 rolled around, with many people hoping that 2000 would be just an average decline. However, Tech stocks and the Dot Com continued their steep decline, affecting the markets early in the year. In the summer, things started to level off a bit, and then September 11, 2001, happened, and the markets went into another tailspin. Figure 3.2 shows how 2001 finished the year down 13.04%, and Rick needed to take out his 5%, so we were down an additional 18.04% for this year on top of the **15.14%** from the previous year. For those of you counting, that is now **33.18%**.

Figure 3.3

Rick was becoming frustrated here but also was a true believer in the markets. No matter what advice was given, he looked back over his 25-year investing life and remembered that he had never seen more than one down year in a row, let alone three, so he wanted to stay in the market. 2002, the war in Iraq and Afghanistan was heating up, and it would take much longer to wrap up. There was also a string of very high-profile bankruptcies in companies like Enron, Global Crossing, KMart, and United Airlines, many of which were due to financial shenanigans. This created another downleg in the stock market, which led to the S&P 500 finishing up the year down **23.37%**. Rick still needed 5% of his rapidly dwindling retirement fund and was now a delivery driver for his brother in Florida. Finishing the year down **28.37%** and **61.55%** by the end of the three years.

By this time, Rick was ready to give in and went to cash in his portfolio, once again our advice. The following year, the market recovered and was up 26.38%.

I tell this story to share an extreme example of what can happen if you pull money from a "diversified" portfolio. Rick's portfolio could have been more diversified (not his choice at the time). Still, many people during this time faired even worse because their portfolios were heavily skewed toward the techs and Dot Coms, down 70-80% after three years.

For me, this was a traumatic period that ended with me being laid off from my job in late 2002 (soon to be hired back). What I learned during this time would affect me for the rest of my career and lead to the creation of what I now call the 3 x 3 Retirement Income Strategy.

Introducing A Better Option

During the early 2000s, my friends and mentors Keith Kruk and Joe Veltri and I began experimenting with different strategies to eliminate some of the issues with retirement income that we had seen in previous years.

Interest rates were at their lowest point since the 1950s, so the bond income strategy was dead. The markets were in turmoil, and clients were shell-shocked and uncomfortable taking risks in the stock market as they had been. There had to be a better way to structure a retirement income plan.

When we look at this strategy from our filter system:

1. **Guarantees:** There are none. You are totally relying on the market for your returns, and as you can see, that can work against you.

2. **Flexibility:** This strategy is undoubtedly flexible and can be changed anytime.

3. **Growth:** This strategy can provide growth over time; however, since income is taken out yearly, withdrawals can magnify negative returns.

As a student of the markets and someone entirely focused on retirees at the time, I never wanted to see what happened to the Ricks of the world again. The aha moment occurred, and the 3 x 3 Retirement Income Strategy™ was born.

The Sure Horizon Retirement Income Strategy™

What I now call the Sure Horizon Retirement Income Strategy™ did not initially have a name. It was the creation of an interdisciplinary team of Insurance Professionals, Financial Planners, and Wealth Managers as a way to take the best of our various professions and build them into a plan that could provide a stable income plan that would not run out of money before the client ran out of life.

Our goal for the plan was simple. It needed to cover essential income needs with guaranteed sources of income while using a minimal amount of assets. It also had to cover and provide for discretionary spending (The Fun Bucket) and be flexible enough to adjust spending in this area. Next, the plan had to give growth to beat inflation over the client's life. More than anything, it needed to make time for the client's friend instead of an enemy.

The result of our experiments became the structure you see below:

Figure 3.4

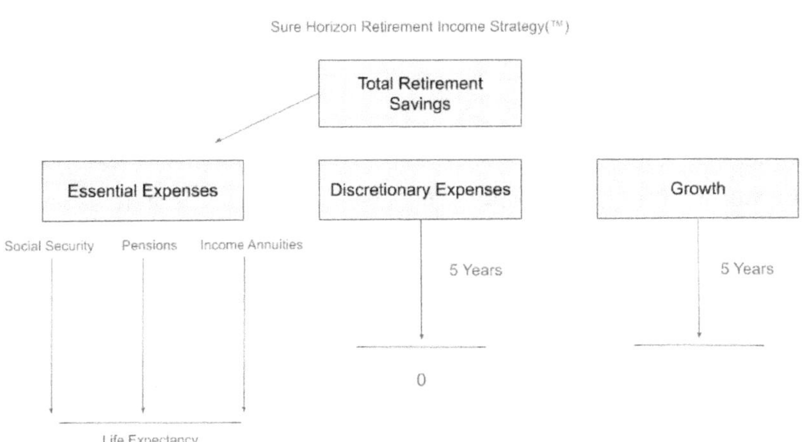

As discussed earlier in this chapter, every plan needs guarantees, Flexibility, and Growth. In addition, it is often better to break your goals into pools of money instead of lumping them together in one portfolio.

Looking at figure 3.4 above, you can see that we have accounted for three separate goals: essential Income, Discretionary Income, and Growth. Each has a different purpose and should be handled differently from an investment standpoint.

In the Essential Income Pool, we want to use Guaranteed Sources of Income: Social Security, Pensions, and Income Annuities. These vehicles place the investment and longevity risk on someone else instead of you, the government, a company, or an insurer.

We want predictability and flexibility for the Discretionary Income Pool, which we typically handle using a bond ladder. The discretionary portion of the portfolio can also be covered by part-time work, a home-based business, or real estate investments. In my designs, we typically run this pool as a five-year sinking fund, meaning it exhausts itself every five years and is funded again.

The final bucket in our plan is the Growth Pool. This pool is designed to provide growth over time to beat inflation. It is from this Growth pool that we will fund our discretionary income goal every 5 years. This pool is the most familiar to you as it is managed similarly to how you have managed your accounts throughout the accumulation phase of life.

I know this doesn't seem easy, but over the next several chapters, we will break it down step by step so that you understand it. By the end of the book, you will be able to design and implement a plan or work with an advisor to do so.

If you would like to see me walk through building a Sure Horizon Retirement Income Strategy™, I have created a 1-hour MasterClass that walks you through creating a plan. You can access this through our companion website at www.Sure-HorizionRetirement.com/Masterclass

Chapter Exercise

This exercise will help you understand how much risk you will take as an investor. In the final chapter, you will complete our retirement income planning workbook, where you will complete a more in-depth version of this exercise.

Determine Your Risk Tolerance

Question 1: How do you feel about market fluctuations?

A) They make me nervous, and I avoid them.

B) I'm cautious but can handle some ups and downs.

C) I'm comfortable with fluctuations as they are part of investing.

Question 2: When thinking about your investments losing value, what's your immediate concern?

A) Losing my money; I might sell to prevent further losses.

B) Concerned but would wait to see if values improve.

C) View it as a natural part of investing and an opportunity to buy more.

Question 3: How do you prefer to invest?

A) Prefer guaranteed or fixed-income investments.

B) A mix of fixed-income and equities.

C) Mostly in equities or other high-growth investments.

Question 4: What is your primary investment goal?

A) Preserve capital; avoid loss.

B) Balance between growth and safety.

C) Maximize returns, accepting higher risks.

Scoring:

Mostly A's: Low-Risk Tolerance

Mostly B's: Moderate Risk Tolerance

Mostly C's: High-Risk Tolerance

This chapter has shown you how you can generate income in retirement. The fixed-income strategy has merits from an investment risk standpoint. Choosing low-risk bonds gives you a predictable income for the bond's life period. However, this type of income portfolio does not consider inflation or reinvestment risks, which can be substantial over a 25+ year retirement.

The Diversified Portfolio strategy is most often used by Brokers and Registered Investment Advisors because their compensation is typically based on assets under management. While it can work and produce the highest returns for a portfolio, it can also have significant market risk and sequence of returns risk. Imagine if it was you instead of Rick, who retired in 2000. Hopefully, you would have been more diversified, but you would still have seen some significant declines in your portfolio during the early 2000s.

For the rest of the book, we will discuss the components and strategies of the Sure Horizon Retirement Income Strategy™. I and a small group of friends have used it for over 25 years with rave client reviews. As an advisor, my clients are happy with their income, enjoy retirement the way they thought they would, and don't spend their lives watching CNBC for the next stock tip or trying to predict when the market will drop. They live life. That is my goal for you. Prepare to plan a secure, flexible, and prosperous retirement for yourself and your family.

Chapter 5

The Role Of Guaranteed Income

"Guaranteed income gives you the peace of mind to pursue your dreams without financial worry."

As we delve into the essential elements of a robust retirement plan, the role of guaranteed income cannot be overstated. Your guaranteed income forms the foundation for a secure and stable retirement, ensuring that the most critical expenses are covered with certainty. But what exactly is guaranteed income, and why is it so crucial?

The Critical Role Covering Essential Expenses

Managing your finances effectively in retirement begins with clearly understanding essential expenses. These costs cover your basic needs and ensure a stable life. Unlike discretionary expenses, which fluctuate based on lifestyle choices, essential expenses are the minimum amounts you need to live comfortably and securely. Let's define what typically falls under this category:

- **Housing:** Whether it's mortgage payments, rent, property taxes, or maintenance fees, housing costs are usually the most significant part of essential expenses.

- **Utilities:** Regular payments for electricity, water, gas, and other utilities are necessary to maintain a safe and comfortable living environment.

- **Food:** This includes all costs associated with groceries and other basic dietary needs.

- **Healthcare:** Often increasing with age, healthcare expenses cover everything from insurance premiums and regular doctor visits to medications and out-of-pocket medical costs.

- **Basic Transportation:** These costs include the costs associated with owning and maintaining a vehicle and public transportation fees if you don't drive.

These expenses are the pillars of a secure retirement. Correctly accounting for them ensures that you can maintain your standard of living without compromising on basic needs. Failure to do this results in lots of sleepless nights and undue worry.

Aligning guaranteed income sources with essential expenses is critical to effective retirement income planning. Guaranteed income — from Social Security, pensions, and income annuities — should ideally cover these fundamental costs. This alignment is crucial because it provides financial stability and reduces the risk of cash flow problems in retirement.

- **Social Security and Pensions:** These are often the primary sources of guaranteed income and are typically designed to replace a portion of your pre-retirement earnings. Understanding how much of your essential expenses these sources can cover is crucial. For many, Social Security benefits are a significant part of their retirement income, specifically structured to adjust for inflation, thus helping to maintain purchasing power as costs rise over the years. For many of you, a pension has never been an option. Or, if you are like me, you might have had a job early on in your career that had one, but you needed to stay longer for it to be of any significance.

- **Income Annuities:** These financial products can be tailored to fill any gaps other income sources leave. By purchasing an annuity, you create an additional layer of guaranteed income that can be specifically allocated towards covering any remaining essential expenses not met by Social Security or pensions. Annuities, like Social Securities and Pensions, can be set up to cover your life or the life of you and your spouse or significant other. This helps to reduce longevity risk, the risk of running out of money before you run out of life.

To ensure that your guaranteed income effectively covers your essential expenses, consider these steps:

1. **Assessment and Planning:** Regularly compare your essential costs against your guaranteed income. This will help you identify any shortfalls early and adjust your financial strategy accordingly.

2. **Budget Management:** Keep a detailed budget that tracks these expenses and your income sources. This practice not only helps you manage your finances more effectively but also allows you to adjust your spending or saving habits as necessary.

Understanding and managing the relationship between guaranteed income and essential expenses is fundamental to ensuring a stable and stress-free retirement. By securing this financial foundation, you can focus on enjoying the more fulfilling aspects of your retirement.

Stability In Your Financial Foundation

In retirement planning, guaranteed income serves as a vital financial safety net. This steady, reliable income stream ensures that essential expenses are consistently covered, providing the peace of mind that your basic needs will always be met, regardless of external economic fluctuations. This foundation of financial stability is crucial, as it frees you from the daily worries over financial survival, allowing you to plan more freely for other fulfilling aspects of your retirement.

The significance of this safety net cannot be understated. It allows for greater flexibility in managing and enjoying discretionary funds, as the fear of being unable to afford basic living costs is largely mitigated. With the assurance that the necessities are secured, you can explore opportunities for travel, hobbies, and other leisure activities that might require financial outlay. You can make these choices without worrying about compromising your essential needs.

Case Studies: The Impact Of Guaranteed Income

To illustrate the transformative impact of guaranteed income, consider the following case studies:

Case Study 1: The Early Retiree

John retired at 62, earlier than many of his peers. He made this decision confidently because his pension plan, savings, and future Social Security (which he held off until 66 to collect) covered all his essential expenses.

Soon after retirement, the economic climate shifted, resulting in increased living costs due to inflation. John had created a bridge investment (buying a short-term 5-year income annuity) that paid the equivalent of his Social Security.

Despite these economic fluctuations, John's guaranteed income from his pension and annuity provided a buffer. This allowed him to adjust his discretionary spending without compromising his quality of life. His guaranteed income and robust safety net made his early retirement secure and fulfilling.

Case Study 2: Navigating Health Challenges

Linda, a retired school teacher, relied on her pension and annuity income to cover her essential expenses.

Early in her retirement, Linda faced unexpected health issues that led to significant medical expenses.

While the medical bills were higher than anticipated, Linda's guaranteed income covered her basic living expenses, allowing her to use her savings to address her healthcare needs without the added stress of funding her day-to-day life. This financial stability gave Linda the peace of mind to focus on her health and recovery rather than worrying about her finances.

Case Study 3: Supporting Family Needs

Robert and his wife Lisa had planned their retirement meticulously, with guaranteed income sources set to cover their essentials.

When their daughter faced a financial crisis, Robert and his wife wanted to help without jeopardizing their financial Security.

Thanks to their stable base of guaranteed income, they were able to assist their daughter through her temporary financial difficulties. The guaranteed income ensured their essential expenses were still met, allowing them to provide support without sacrificing their financial well-being.

These scenarios underscore guaranteed income's fundamental role in providing a reliable financial foundation in retirement. It covers essential costs and acts as a protective buffer against life's unpredictable occurrences. This stability is indispensable, as it secures a retiree's present financial needs and fortifies their ability to handle unforeseen challenges, thereby enhancing their overall quality of life during retirement.

Diversifying Sources Of Guaranteed Income

Having multiple guaranteed income streams in retirement can significantly enhance your financial Security. Let's explore the main sources of guaranteed income—Social Security, pensions, and income annuities—each offering unique benefits and considerations.

Social Security

Social Security is a foundational pillar for most American retirees, providing inflation-adjusted payments for life. The key to maximizing Social Security benefits lies in strategic timing. Delaying the start of benefits until full retirement age or even up to age 70 can significantly increase your monthly payout. For married couples, coordinating claims to optimize benefits—such as one spouse claiming early while the other delays—can maximize lifetime benefits. Individuals with health concerns might consider claiming earlier to ensure they receive benefits for a more extended period, even though the monthly amount might be lower.

Pensions

Pensions provide a fixed income, typically based on your salary and years of service. They offer a predictable, stable income with no investment risk for retirees. However, pensions are less flexible, and their safety depends heavily on the employer's financial health. Understanding the terms of your pension—whether it offers options like a lump sum or lifetime annuity payments—is crucial for integrating this income into your broader financial plan.

Income Annuities

Income annuities are insurance products that convert a lump sum payment into a regular income stream, providing stability regardless of market conditions. These can be structured as immediate annuities that start paying almost immediately or deferred annuities that begin payments at a future date and allow the investment to grow. The choice between immediate and deferred annuities should align with your cash flow needs. Adding riders for inflation protection or survivor benefits can tailor an annuity to fit your retirement strategy more closely.

Integrating Multiple Sources

The art of retirement planning involves aligning these diverse income sources with your projected expenses. Social Security and pensions are best suited for covering immediate and essential expenses due to their stability and predictability. In contrast, income annuities are adaptable and can be structured to meet future financial needs, providing an excellent way to ensure longevity protection.

By thoughtfully combining these income streams, retirees can create a well-rounded financial safety net that covers all necessary expenses and adjusts to life's changes, offering peace of mind and financial stability throughout retirement. This integrated approach ensures that each part of your retirement plan works together seamlessly, allowing you to enjoy a secure and worry-free retirement.

Guaranteeing Your Financial Independence

When your basic needs are securely funded, you can focus on pursuits that enrich your life. Whether it's traveling to places you've always dreamed of visiting, investing time in hobbies you've been eager to explore, or simply enjoying leisure activities with friends and family, the assurance of guaranteed income supports these ventures. This financial independence is invaluable as it enhances your quality of life and allows you to maximize your retirement years.

While setting up guaranteed income streams is a significant first step toward a secure retirement, it is equally important to maintain a proactive approach by regularly reviewing and adjusting your strategies. Life is not static; your retirement plan should be dynamic enough to adapt to changes.

- **Adapting to Legal and Economic Changes:** Changes in laws and fluctuations in the economic climate can impact benefits and the value of your investments. For instance, modifications to Social Security policies or pension adjustments necessitate reviewing your financial strategies to ensure they remain adequate.

- **Personal Circumstances:** Your needs and circumstances can change as you progress through retirement. Health considerations may alter the cost of your medical care, or you might decide to move closer to family, impacting your living expenses. Regular assessments allow you to adjust your plans to accommodate these changes, ensuring your income streams continue to meet your needs.

- **Strategy Reviews:** Set a schedule to review your income streams and expenses annually or whenever a significant change in your life or the broader financial landscape exists. Whether done by you or working with a financial advisor, these reviews can help you identify potential issues before they become problematic and adjust your plans to continue meeting your goals efficiently.

Chapter Exercise

Exercise: Calculate Your Guaranteed Income

Objective: This exercise helps you to calculate the total guaranteed income you can expect from all sources and compare this to your list of essential expenses. This is a critical step in ensuring your basic needs are consistently met throughout retirement.

Instructions:

List Your Sources: List all guaranteed income sources, such as Social Security, pensions, and income annuities.

Monthly Income: Next to each source, write down the monthly income you expect to receive from it. If you need more clarification, use estimates based on your latest statements or online calculators for Social Security.

Total It Up: Add the monthly figures for your guaranteed monthly income.

Compare Against Expenses: Compare this total to your monthly essential expenses calculated previously (housing, utilities, food, healthcare, basic transportation). This comparison will help you see if your guaranteed income covers all your essential costs or if there's a shortfall you need to address.

Outcome: Completing this exercise will provide you with a clear understanding of how well your essential living costs are covered by guaranteed income, highlighting areas where you may need to adjust your planning or consider additional income sources.

Objective: The Guaranteed Income Planner worksheet is designed to help you organize and plan your guaranteed income streams effectively, considering the timing of benefits and the amount expected from each source.

Final Thoughts

Guaranteed income is more than just a financial safety net; it is the cornerstone of a fulfilling and independent retirement. By understanding and effectively managing these income sources, you ensure your financial security and ability to live on your terms. Regularly revisiting and refining your income strategies is crucial in maintaining this independence, allowing you to adapt to the ever-changing landscape of life and finance.

As we close this chapter, remember that planning for retirement is an ongoing journey. Today's steps to secure and manage your guaranteed income will set the stage for a vibrant, engaging, and worry-free retirement. In the next chapter, we will look at the next element of a thriving income plan: Flexibility.

Chapter 6

Staying Flexible and Adapting To Change

"Flexibility in retirement planning isn't a luxury—it's a necessity."

Retirement planning isn't just about putting your finances on autopilot once you retire. It's about creating a flexible, adaptive plan that can evolve with your needs and the changing economic landscape. Think of flexibility as a cornerstone of your retirement strategy. With it, you can stay afloat amid unexpected challenges or seize new opportunities.

Dynamic Nature of Retirement

Retirement isn't static; it's dynamic, often spanning two to three decades. Over this period, your needs, lifestyle, and market conditions will likely shift. That once-perfect retirement plan might not remain relevant throughout your retirement journey. Adapting your strategy is essential to keep pace with your evolving goals and ensure long-term financial security and personal satisfaction.

Adapting to Different Life Phases

In retirement, life unfolds in phases:

- **The Active Early Years:** This phase is characterized by travel, new hobbies, and vibrant social activities. Discretionary spending is typically higher.

- **The Settled Middle Years**: Energy levels might dip, and your interests may shift. Discretionary expenses may decrease while healthcare costs start to rise.

- **The Golden Later Years:** Mobility and health issues might limit activities, and healthcare costs often become the primary expense.

Flexibility Is Key

Maintaining flexibility means regularly reviewing your retirement plan and adjusting as needed. It's about staying resilient and ensuring your plan aligns with your goals. This chapter will explore strategies and tools for staying flexible and adapting to changes as you progress through retirement.

Flexible planning is crucial for a resilient and adaptive retirement strategy. You can confidently navigate life's twists and turns by regularly assessing and updating your retirement plan and employing adaptive strategies like adjusting withdrawal rates or changing asset allocations.

Retirement is a dynamic phase, and personal circumstances can change unexpectedly. Here's how to adapt your plan when life throws you a curveball.

In early retirement, you should spend more money on discretionary spending. While your health is still good, knock those things off your "Bucket List" that will require mobility and health.

I remember when my parents retired. The first five years, they focused on visiting places that required them to travel long distances and required physical effort. They are big cruisers who made long trips to South America and the Far East. Many of these trips required as much as 14-20 hours on a plane and required physical effort, like visiting Machu Pichu and climbing the Great Wall of China. In their 60s, this was demanding. Today, in their 70s and 80s, it isn't easy to get them to travel more than three hours in a car to come visit us.

My advice to my clients is to make sure they have a bucket list of places to go and things they want to do before retirement and then build a plan that funds those for at least the first five years. After that, adjust the plan accordingly every five years going forward.

Health Changes

Health changes can significantly impact your retirement plan, both financially and emotionally. From a healthcare perspective, you must have several things locked down before and when you get into retirement.

First, you must make sure your Medicare or private health insurance plans cover your current health needs. If you retire before age 65, you must have some form of private healthcare. Some companies may provide Retiree health insurance, but this is becoming rarer each year like pensions. If you do have it, continuing coverage through your company can be expensive.

For those under age 65, not only are marketplace plans available, but today, coverage is also available through other healthcare providers, such as medical share plans that can be more comprehensive yet less expensive than traditional healthcare. It is advisable to spend some time learning about your options and consulting with a healthcare advisor skilled at both traditional health insurance and alternative plans.

When you reach the age of 65, even if you are still working, you will need to sign up for Medicare. Medicare comes in two main parts: Medicare A and Medicare B, as well as prescription drug coverage through Medicare D. While A & B cover the high dollar costs of retirement, you may want to consider adding a Medigap or Medicare Advantage plan to give you additional benefits and defray some of the out of pocket costs. Consider working with a Medicare Advisor; in most cases, you will not pay any extra for them, and they will help you navigate all the available plans and can customize a plan based on your health needs.

Long-Term Care Planning

We will all get older and certainly reach a point where we might need either home care or some type of facility later in life. This can become extremely expensive if you are not prepared for it. Once you reach 55+, you should investigate. You have a 60% chance of needing long-term care during your life, according to LongTermCare.gov. That rate exceeds your need to use your Homeowner's and Auto Coverage. I have added a particular bonus chapter on long-term care at the end of the book.

As you start planning your retirement budget, healthcare should be a significant part of it. Include regular doctor visits, prescription medications, and potential out-of-pocket expenses in your healthcare budget. Account for inflation in healthcare costs over time. Medical Inflation rates have trended higher than core inflation over the last 14 years and are projected to stay at those rates for the foreseeable future.

Estate Planning and Legal Documents

As you prepare for retirement, consider reviewing your estate planning and legal documents to ensure they are up-to-date and flexible as your life changes. The core Estate Planning Documents that you should have in place are:

1. **Will:** Legal document outlining the distribution of assets after death. It names guardians for minor children and specifies beneficiaries and their inheritances. Appoints an executor to manage the estate. Can include specific bequests, charitable donations, and funeral instructions

2. **Durable Power of Attorney (DPOA):** Allows a designated agent to handle financial and legal matters on behalf of the principal. Remains effective even if the principal becomes incapacitated. Authorizes the agent to manage bank accounts, pay bills, buy/sell property, etc. The DPOA can be immediate or "springing" (only effective upon incapacity).

3. **Medical Power of Attorney (MPOA):** A designated agent can make healthcare decisions if the principal (the Grantor) cannot do so. Grants the agent's authority over medical treatment, surgeries, and other healthcare decisions. Requires compliance with the principal's known wishes or best interests.

4. **Directive to Physician (Living Will):** Outlines a person's preferences regarding end-of-life medical treatment. Guides healthcare professionals and family members when the individual cannot communicate their wishes. Includes preferences for life-sustaining treatment like resuscitation, mechanical ventilation, and artificial nutrition/hydration. Can specify organ donation wishes.

5. **Trust:** Legal arrangement in which a trustee manages assets for beneficiaries. It can help avoid probate, provide for minor children, and protect assets from

creditors.

a. **Types and Features:**

- **Revocable Living Trusts** Can be amended or revoked by the Grantor. They provide flexibility and asset management during life and after death.

- **Irrevocable Trust:** This cannot be changed once established. Offers potential tax benefits and asset protection

- **Special Needs Trust:** Provides for disabled beneficiaries without affecting government benefits.

Family Dynamics

Family changes can dramatically shift your retirement needs, whether you're supporting adult children or caring for an aging parent.

When it comes to your adult children, it is essential to establish boundaries. Determine the type and extent of financial assistance you can provide without jeopardizing your retirement goals. Encourage them to take responsibility for their financial future. Remember that the money you have saved and set aside for yourself is all you have. Giving that money to adult children can put you in a financial predicament.

Assuming Caregiving Responsibilities

One of our generation's challenges in the current economic environment is that our kids who are getting started in their careers may need financial assistance or continue living at home. However, our Leading-Edge Boomer Parents and Grandparents who are experiencing some of the challenges of our high-inflation economy may also need help and assistance. The challenge for us is that we plan for our own retirements.

Your retirement plan must adapt to life's changing circumstances, especially unexpected health issues or family dynamics. By being proactive and flexible, you can adjust your retirement strategy to ensure you continue living a fulfilling and financially secure life.

Navigating Market Conditions

When the market starts dipping, and your portfolio looks like it's on a rollercoaster, it's easy to let your emotions take the wheel. But that's the worst thing you can do. Here's how to keep a cool head when the markets get turbulent.

Emotional Resilience Strategies

- **Stay Calm and Stick to the Plan:** Feeling nervous when the market's plummeting faster than a skydiver without a parachute is natural. However, remember that market volatility is part and parcel of investing. Think long-term. If you've got a solid plan, stick to it. Making sudden changes because the media screams "sell!" won't do you any favors.

- **Avoid Panic Selling:** Selling investments during a market downturn is like jumping off a sinking ship without checking if the water is shallow. You might survive the fall, but you're likely to regret it. Before you make any drastic moves, call your financial advisor for a reality check.

- **Review Historical Market Trends:** Look back at history. Every downturn eventually rebounded. From the Great Depression to the Great Recession, markets have recovered repeatedly. Corrections, bear markets, and recessions are temporary—they're bumps in the road, not dead ends.

Technical Strategies to Protect Your Portfolio

- **Diversify Your Investments:** Don't put all your eggs in one basket. Spread your investments across asset classes like stocks, bonds, and real estate. And remember international diversification. U.S. markets are great, but there are other games in town.

- **Use Stop-Loss Orders:** A stop-loss order can automatically sell your investments if they drop below a certain value. Think of it as your portfolio's emergency brake. This strategy helps limit losses, especially during sudden downturns.

- **Rebalance Your Portfolio:** Rebalancing is like tuning up your car. You want to ensure your portfolio sticks to the planned asset allocation so it's not over-exposed to risky assets. Market dips can be an opportunity to buy undervalued investments, and rebalancing lets you do just that.

- **Consider Low-Volatility Funds:** Want a smoother ride? Low-volatility funds invest in companies with stable earnings and low debt. They're designed to minimize market fluctuations and can help you sleep better at night when the markets are shaky.

Economic Changes

Significant economic shifts, like inflation spikes and interest rate swings, can seriously impact your retirement strategy. Here's how to stay on top of your game.

Inflation Spikes

- **Inflation-Protected Securities:** Treasury Inflation-Protected Securities (TIPS) and Series I Savings Bonds are like kryptonite for inflation. TIPS are indexed to inflation, so your investment's value keeps up with rising prices. Series I Savings Bonds work similarly, offering inflation protection.

- **Tangible Assets:** Inflation eats into your buying power, but tangible assets like real estate and commodities can help you fight back. Real Estate Investment Trusts (REITs) and commodity ETFs are easy ways to add tangible assets to your portfolio.

- **Dividend Growth Stocks:** Companies with a track record of increasing dividends year after year can be your inflation-fighting friends. Think utilities, consumer staples, and healthcare – sectors where demand doesn't take a nosedive, even when prices rise.

Interest Rate Fluctuations

- **Bond Ladder Strategy:** A bond ladder is like having multiple safety nets. By staggering bond maturities over time, you create a steady income stream while reducing reinvestment risk when rates are low. It's an intelligent way to manage interest rate risks. We use a Bond Ladder Strategy for the Discretionary Income Pool of the 3 x 3 Retirement Income Strategy that you will learn about in the upcoming chapters.

- **Short-Duration Bonds:** Short-duration bonds don't feel the pain of rising interest rates like their long-term cousins. They're less sensitive to rate changes, so they can help cushion your portfolio when the Federal Reserve decides to play hardball.

- **Floating-Rate Bonds:** Floating-rate bonds have interest rates that adjust with the market. When rates rise, so do the yields on these bonds. Bank loan funds can also offer higher yields at a rising rate.

Dealing with market volatility and economic changes isn't just about managing your investments – it's about managing your emotions, too. By staying calm, sticking to your plan, and employing intelligent strategies like diversification, rebalancing, and inflation-proofing your portfolio, you'll be ready to handle whatever the market throws at you.

Wrapping Up

Retirement isn't a straight line from point A to point B. It's more like a scenic route filled with unexpected twists, pit stops, and the occasional detour. But that's the beauty of it! Flexibility and adaptability are your secret weapons for successful retirement planning.

Instead of dreading changes, consider them opportunities to refine and improve your plan. Whether it's a market dip, a health challenge, or a sudden windfall, adapting your strategy ensures you're always steering toward your goals.

It's time to take the wheel! Schedule regular reviews of your retirement plan and stay proactive in adapting to life's changes. Mark your calendar for a quarterly or annual review. And don't be shy about seeking advice from a trusted financial advisor to ensure you remain well-prepared for the future.

Here's a little mantra to keep in mind: Adapt. Plan. Prosper.

The next chapter will explore how growth should be part of every retirement plan.

Chapter 7

The Importance Of Growth In Retirement

"Growth isn't optional; it's essential. Your retirement plan must outpace inflation to secure your future."

As we discuss the importance of Growth during retirement, it's crucial to recognize why nurturing the Growth of your retirement funds is not just beneficial but essential. The need for Growth stems from a fundamental reality—our increasing life expectancies and the continuous erosion of purchasing power due to inflation. Without a growth component in your retirement plan, there's a real risk that your funds could deplete faster than anticipated, potentially leaving you financially vulnerable later in life.

Why Growth Matters

Think of your retirement funds as a living entity that must grow and adapt to an ever-changing economic landscape. With retirees today enjoying longer lifespans than previous generations, the demand for retirement savings is more significant. Here's why ensuring these funds continue to grow is critical:

- **Longevity Risk:** As life expectancies increase, so does the period your retirement savings need to cover. Without Growth, there's a higher risk of outliving your savings, which can lead to financial strain in later years.

- **Inflation:** Inflation gradually erodes the value of money over time, decreasing your purchasing power. You can maintain your living standard if your retirement income keeps up with inflation.

Balancing Safety with Growth

While the need for Growth is evident, balancing this with safety is equally important—primarily when relying on your savings for daily living expenses. The challenge is finding a strategy that offers a good mix of safety and growth potential.

- **Strategic Approach:** Adopting a strategic approach to your investments can help manage the risks of seeking Growth. This is why we treat the growth component of the 3 x 3 Retirement Income Strategy as a separate component with a 5-year strategy. That allows us to ride out most market downturns. We will look at this more in detail in the Growth Pool chapter.

- **Risk Mitigation:** One key strategy is diversification across different types of investments. By spreading your investments across stocks, bonds, real estate, and other assets, you can capture growth opportunities while mitigating the risk of major losses.

- **Future Needs:** It's also vital to consider the timing of your needs. While more conservative investments might be appropriate as you near retirement, keeping a portion of your portfolio in growth-oriented investments can be wise, especially if you have a longer time horizon.

As we delve deeper into this chapter, we will explore specific strategies and investment types to help you achieve a balanced approach to growing and safeguarding your retirement funds. The goal is to ensure that your retirement savings not only support you in the present but also continue to thrive, providing you with financial security and peace of mind throughout your retirement years.

Understanding The Growth Pool

In retirement planning, Growth represents a crucial segment of your investment portfolio, specifically earmarked for long-term Growth. Think of it as the part of your garden where you plant seeds that will take longer to mature but ultimately bear the most fruit. This pool is not just about increasing your wealth; it's about strategic replenishment and sustainability.

The primary aim of this pool is to provide a financial reservoir to replenish funds used for discretionary spending and to cover unexpected long-term expenses that may arise. It acts as a financial safeguard, ensuring that you have the means to support your lifestyle not just now but well into the future.

The Growth Pool is not an isolated element; it's an integral part of your broader retirement income strategy. Its role is to complement your immediate income sources, such as Social Security, pensions, and annuities, by offering financial Growth and security that extends the lifespan of your overall portfolio.

By strategically growing this segment of your portfolio, you ensure a continuous flow of funds available when your more immediate income sources might be depleting. It's like having a well that refills itself, providing you with financial water to draw from as needed.

The Growth Pool is a financial backstop, growing over time and providing a buffer against inflation and other economic changes that can erode fixed income sources. This pool allows for financial flexibility and security, giving you peace of mind that your needs will be met, even as market conditions fluctuate.

Growth is essential to a holistic retirement strategy to ensure long-term financial health and sustainability. You secure your future and balance enjoying your present and planning for your future needs. In the following sections, we'll explore how to manage and optimize the Growth Pool to maximize its benefits and ensure it serves its purpose effectively within your retirement planning framework.

Strategies For Growing Retirement Funds

One of the critical components of any Growth Strategy is Asset Allocation. Asset allocation is much like crafting the perfect blend of coffee—get it right, and it's delightful; mess it up, and you might be in for some sleepless nights. In the early days of your retirement, you can likely afford to be a bit bold, keeping a substantial chunk of your portfolio in stocks to encourage Growth. But as you journey into retirement, or if economic storms brew, shifting more into bonds or other steadier investments might save you from financial heartache.

Consider how a seasoned sailor adjusts the sails to the changing winds—your investment strategy should similarly adapt to life's ongoing shifts and the economic climate. It's about maintaining balance: too much risk might capsize your financial security, and too little might leave you stalled with insufficient Growth.

Another critical component of Growth is Diversification. Diversification is your strategy for not putting all your eggs in one basket. It's about spreading your investments across various asset types to capture opportunities wherever they arise and, more importantly, to cushion against the fall if one sector or market takes a hit.

Imagine your portfolio as a team of athletes; you want a diversified group where each plays a unique role. Some are steady and reliable, like your bonds. In contrast, others, like stocks in emerging markets or new sectors, have the potential to sprint ahead, bringing in hefty rewards. Spreading your investments like this helps manage risk and positions you to benefit from Growth in unexpected quarters.

Leveraging Tax-Advantaged Accounts

Using tax-advantaged accounts like Roth IRAs or 401(k)s is about being as innovative with your taxes as your investments. These accounts offer significant tax breaks that can have a compound effect on your retirement savings growth. With a Roth IRA, for example, your investments grow tax-free, and you don't owe a penny in taxes on withdrawals, which can significantly enhance your financial position in retirement.

Think of it this way: strategically planning which accounts to draw from first can maximize your investment growth and minimize tax liabilities. Let your tax-advantaged accounts compound for longer. In that case, you supercharge your retirement fund without putting in extra cash.

Growing your retirement funds isn't just about picking investments—crafting a sophisticated strategy that evolves with your retirement journey. Your financial plan should mirror your life's path, becoming more conservative as you seek stability or take advantage of growth opportunities. Remember, this is about ensuring your financial engine doesn't just keep running. Still, it runs well, so you can enjoy your retirement without worrying about financial instability.

Adjusting Your Growth Pool Over Time

Keeping your Growth Pool in tune is crucial as you navigate through retirement. It's like tuning a musical instrument—regular adjustments ensure it sounds right. Monitoring and rebalancing your investments periodically ensures that your portfolio aligns with your retirement goals and risk tolerance.

Rebalancing isn't just about numbers; it's about keeping your financial goals on track. As markets rise and fall, the actual allocation of your assets can drift from your intended target. For example, if equities have done well, they might now represent a more significant portion of your portfolio than you originally planned, exposing you to higher risk than you're comfortable with. Rebalancing helps you sell off some of those equities and buy more bonds, realigning your portfolio with your risk tolerance and long-term objectives.

Responding to Market Changes

The financial markets are like the weather—constantly changing, sometimes predictably, sometimes not. Having strategies to adjust your Growth Pool in response to these changes is like having a good weather plan on a sailing trip.

When markets dip, it might seem counterintuitive. Still, it can be an opportune time to buy high-quality assets at a discount—think of it as a sale on your favorite brand. Conversely, when markets are riding high, it might be a good time to trim or sell assets that have become overvalued, locking in gains and reducing risk. This kind of strategic adjustment can significantly enhance the longevity and health of your Growth Pool.

Making these adjustments requires a keen eye and a steady hand. It's not about reacting to every market blip but about making thoughtful, strategic changes based on broader economic conditions and personal retirement timelines. Always ensure that any changes align with your retirement strategy and risk tolerance. This approach allows you to navigate market volatility confidently, ensuring your retirement funds continue to grow and support you throughout your golden years.

Adjusting your Growth Pool over time is essential for maintaining financial health in retirement. Just as a gardener prunes and nurtures a garden to achieve the best bloom, so must you monitor, rebalance, and adjust your investments to ensure they continue to meet your needs and goals. With careful attention and regular adjustments, your Growth Pool can flourish, providing financial security and peace of mind in retirement.

Case Studies

Case Study 1: Diversification Triumph – Linda's Story

Linda, having retired at 65, found that her investment portfolio was excessively concentrated in high-volatility tech stocks. While these had served her well during her working years, the high risk associated with a tech-heavy portfolio was unsuitable for her retirement, especially with her desire for a stable income and lower risk of capital erosion.

Strategies Used:

Linda worked with her financial advisor to diversify her investments to address this. They reduced her exposure to tech stocks and increased her holdings in more stable assets like bonds, real estate investment trusts (REITs), and a select mix of utilities and consumer goods stocks. They also introduced a small but strategic allocation to commodities as a hedge against inflation.

End Result:

This diversification strategy helped stabilize Linda's income streams and reduced the overall volatility of her portfolio. As a result, she enjoyed a more consistent return, which supported her living expenses without forcing her to sell assets during market downturns. Over the first five years of her retirement, her portfolio achieved balanced Growth of 7% per year, aligning perfectly with her needs for stability and modest Growth.

Case Study 2: Strategic Rebalancing – Jim's Approach

Jim entered retirement with a robust portfolio predominantly invested in equities. While the aggressive growth strategy had accelerated his savings pre-retirement, the high exposure to stock market fluctuations became a significant concern as he sought more predictability and safety in his income sources.

Strategies Used:

Jim and his financial planner decided on a gradual rebalancing strategy. They would shift some of the equity holdings each year into bonds and fixed-income securities. They focused mainly on corporate and municipal bonds to benefit from favorable tax treatments. Additionally, they scheduled semi-annual portfolio reviews to adjust the asset allocation based on current market conditions and Jim's evolving risk tolerance.

End Result:

Over several years, Jim's portfolio transitioned from a high-risk to a more conservative profile, significantly reducing the impact of market dips on its overall value. This shift preserved his capital and provided him with predictable income streams. Jim's portfolio delivered an average annual growth rate of 6% with reduced volatility, thus securing his financial needs throughout retirement.

Case Study 3: Navigating Market Changes – Susan's Dynamic Strategy

Susan, a recent retiree, was initially invested heavily in fixed-income securities. However, with the onset of a low-interest-rate environment, the yields on her investments began to decline, threatening her expected retirement income.

Strategies Used:

Susan reacted to the changing market conditions by reallocating her investment focus. She reduced her percentage in low-yield bonds and increased her stake in dividend-paying stocks and sector-specific ETFs that targeted industries less affected by economic downturns, such as healthcare and technology. She also invested a portion of her portfolio in high-growth potential startups using a well-regulated crowdfunding platform.

End Result:

Susan's adjustments allowed her to enhance her income through higher dividend yields and potential capital gains from her equity investments. The startups presented a riskier venture but paid off, contributing to an overall annual portfolio growth of 6%, comfortably offsetting the lower bond yields. Her proactive approach ensured that her retirement savings maintained their purchasing power and saw appreciable Growth despite challenging economic conditions.

These case studies illustrate that effective management of the Growth Pool involves a mix of strategic planning, timely rebalancing, and a proactive response to market conditions. By understanding these real-life applications, retirees can better adapt their strategies to meet their long-term financial goals, ensuring a stable and fulfilling retirement.

Conclusion: Why Growth Matters

This chapter covers a lot of ground, centered around one key idea: growth. Retirement isn't just about ensuring you have enough to get by; it's about ensuring your savings can go the distance while letting you live your best life.

Let's recap the essentials, but in plain, simple terms:

First, we tackled why Growth matters. People are living longer than ever, and inflation is like a thief slowly draining your purchasing power. With Growth, your retirement savings might last longer to fund your envisioned lifestyle. You want your money to work as hard for you now as you did for it during your career.

Then, we dug into the concept of the Growth Pool. This pool is your long-term safety net—where you stash a portion of your savings specifically to grow over time. It's the financial backstop that keeps your retirement income plan intact, even if life throws some surprises your way.

Next, we discussed the strategies for growing your retirement funds:

- **Asset Allocation** is the process of finding the right balance between stocks, bonds, and other investments to match one's goals and risk tolerance.

- **Diversification**: Spreading your money across different sectors, assets, and regions so you're not relying too heavily on one particular basket.

- **Tax-Advantaged Accounts**: Using Roth IRAs and 401(k)s to let your money grow tax-free and ensure every dollar you save is working its hardest.

Adjusting the Growth Pool over time is crucial. Markets change, and so should your strategy. Keeping an eye on your investments and regularly rebalancing them ensures they align with your goals. And when markets shift, you need to be ready to pivot. Sometimes, it's about taking advantage of market downturns to buy quality assets cheaply; other times, it's about protecting your nest egg from unnecessary risk.

We examined some real-world scenarios through our case studies to bring it all home. Linda, Jim, and Susan each had unique challenges, but using smart strategies like diversification and rebalancing kept their retirement funds growing and secure.

So, what's the takeaway here?

Maintaining Growth in retirement isn't just a "nice-to-have"; it's essential. It requires intelligence, flexibility, and strategic thinking. Building your Growth Pool strategy right will give you the peace of mind and financial security you need to live your best retirement life.

Next, we'll examine three main components of your essential income strategy, Social Security.

Chapter 8

Navigating Social Security

"Understanding how Social Security works is essential for anyone planning for retirement."

As we dive into the intricacies of Social Security, a concern that often looms large in the minds of many is the future health and viability of the system itself. In a landscape where headlines frequently cast doubt on the longevity of Social Security funds, it's natural to wonder: will the benefits be there when I retire? "

The Backbone of the American Retirement System

Since its inception in 1935, Social Security has been more than just a government program; it's a fundamental pillar of economic security for millions of aging Americans, disabled individuals, and survivors. Funded through payroll taxes, this program provides a basic income for those who have spent decades in the workforce and adjusts these benefits for inflation, a feature not commonly found in private retirement plans.

Addressing the Elephant in The Room: Will Social Security Run Out?

The biggest question I hear from clients is, "Will Social Security run out?" While it's true that Social Security faces funding challenges, primarily due to an aging population and a shrinking ratio of workers to beneficiaries, it's more dire than some rumors suggest. According to the most recent reports from the Social Security Administration, the trust funds that support Social Security are expected to pay out in full until 2035. Post-2035, even with no changes to the system, incoming payroll taxes are projected to cover about 79% of scheduled benefits. Here is my take on the system. Congress will drag its feet until it gets severe and then fix the problem. What politician is going to be responsible for the death of Social Security? The government has the ability to print any money it needs to pay the bills. Don't let the dysfunction of Washington scare you.

The takeaway isn't just to plan for Social Security to vanish but to understand how to maximize what you're entitled to under the current laws. It's also a call to action to plan comprehensively for retirement, considering other income streams and savings strategies. As we discuss the workings of Social Security, from determining eligibility to calculating benefits, remember that while Social Security is an essential part of retirement planning, it should be one piece of your overall retirement puzzle.

Navigating Through Uncertainty

In this chapter, I will equip you with the knowledge to navigate the complexities of Social Security, ensuring you understand how to claim the maximum benefits you are entitled to. We'll also delve into strategic decisions around the timing of benefits and how to integrate this critical source of income with other retirement planning elements. This will help you maximize your financial security and provide peace of mind, knowing you have a strategy that accounts for various scenarios.

So, let's clear the fog surrounding Social Security and lay down the strategies that ensure you can rely on this vital safety net, adapting your plans to whatever the future holds.

Understanding How Social Security Works

Understanding how Social Security works is essential for anyone planning their retirement, as it impacts when and how they can access their benefits and the amount they receive.

Social Security benefits are calculated based on an individual's work history and career earnings. The Social Security Administration (SSA) uses the average indexed monthly earnings (AIME) over the 35 highest earning years of a worker's career to calculate the Primary Insurance Amount (PIA), which is the basis for the benefits calculations.

The age at which you start claiming Social Security benefits significantly affects your monthly benefit amount. You can begin receiving benefits as early as age 62, but taking benefits before your full retirement age (FRA) permanently reduces benefits. On the other hand, delaying benefits past your FRA up to age 70 can increase your monthly benefits, thanks to delayed retirement credits.

This comprehensive system ensures that Social Security functions as a dynamic support structure, adapting to the various needs of retirees, disabled workers, and families of deceased workers. Understanding these mechanics is crucial for anyone looking to maximize their benefits and effectively integrate Social Security into their retirement strategy. As we proceed, we'll explore techniques for optimizing your Social Security benefits, considering factors like marital status, health, and other personal circumstances.

Social Security is one of the most critical components of America's retirement planning landscape. Established by President Franklin D. Roosevelt in 1935 during the New Deal era, It was designed as a safety net to support older adults, disabled individuals, and survivors of deceased workers. Its primary purpose is to provide these groups a continuous source of income, ensuring they can maintain a basic standard of living despite the loss of employment income due to age, disability, or death.

The program is funded through payroll taxes collected from workers and their employers, known as the Federal Insurance Contributions Act (FICA) tax. This structure underpins a social insurance program that contributes to the economic security of millions of Americans, making it a vital element of national social policy.

Determining Eligibility

Navigating the maze of Social Security eligibility is akin to decoding a complex puzzle. Still, it's a puzzle that holds the key to your financial security in retirement. Let's break down what it takes to qualify for Social Security benefits, shall we?

Work Credits: Your Ticket To Benefits

Think of credits as your admission ticket to the Social Security party. You'll need 40 tickets, translating to about 10 years of work. You earn these credits as you pay into the system, with one credit in 2021 earned for every $1,470 in wages or self-employment income. You can only earn up to four credits per year, so plan your career duration accordingly.

Age Requirements

The earliest age you can start receiving Social Security retirement benefits is 62. However, each individual has a "full retirement age" (FRA) based on their birth year, which ranges from 66 to 67 for those born after 1943. Claiming benefits before reaching your FRA results in a reduction of your monthly benefit.

You can delay receiving benefits past your FRA until age 70, which increases your monthly benefit amount. Every year you take it before your full retirement age, you lose 7.6%. Every year that you wait beyond FRA, you will gain 7.6% per year.

Calculating Your Benefits

The Social Security Administration calculates your benefits based on your lifetime earnings, adjusted for inflation. The SSA takes your 35 highest earning years, adjusts them for inflation, and averages them to find your AIME.

The next step is to determine your Primary Insurance Amount (PIA). The PIA is the sum of three separate percentages of portions of your AIME. The portions are defined by "bend points" that change yearly.

For example, in 2021, the formula is 90% of the first $996 of your AIME, 32% between $996 and $6,002, and 15% of any amount over $6,002.

This calculation provides the monthly amount you would receive if you start benefits at your full retirement age.

This seems complex, which it is. The good news is you can log on to your account at SSA.gov and get the different amounts based on when you plan to retire.

Strategies For Maximizing Your Benefits

Maximizing your Social Security benefits involves understanding and strategically planning around several vital factors. Let's delve into how timing your benefits, considering marital status, and learning from real-life scenarios can enhance your financial stability during retirement.

Timing Your Benefits

Deciding When to Start Receiving Benefits:

- **Early Retirement:** You can start receiving Social Security benefits at age 62, but doing so will reduce your monthly benefit amount for life. For example, if your full retirement age (FRA) is 67, claiming 62 will reduce your benefits by about 30%.

- **Full Retirement Age (FRA):** Claiming at your FRA allows you to receive your total benefit amount. The FRA varies depending on your birth year, ranging from 66 to 67 for most people today.

- **Delayed Retirement:** You can delay your benefits beyond your FRA until age 70. For each year you delay, your benefits increase by approximately 7.6%. This increase stops once you reach age 70, providing a significantly higher monthly benefit for the rest of your life.

Starting benefits early might be necessary if you need income immediately or have health concerns that could shorten your life expectancy.

Delaying benefits is advantageous if you have other income sources and are healthy. It increases your monthly payout and potentially your overall lifetime benefits. The advantage is that you have a more extensive base from which to start for cost of living adjustments (COLA).

Marital Status Considerations

Strategies Based on Marital Status:

- **Married Couples:** Coordination is critical. One common strategy is for the higher earner to delay benefits to maximize the survivor benefit. In comparison, the lower earner might start benefits earlier.

- **Divorced Individuals:** If you were married for at least 10 years, you might be eligible for benefits based on your ex-spouse's work record, provided you haven't remarried.

- **Widows/Widowers:** Survivor benefits allow you to claim benefits on your deceased spouse's record. You can start these as early as 60, but they will be reduced if claimed before your full retirement age.

Implications of Remarriage:

Remarrying can affect your eligibility for spousal or survivor benefits from a previous marriage. Understanding these rules is crucial to plan effectively and maintain your benefit options.

Real-Life Scenarios

Scenario 1: Early vs. Delayed Benefits

Jim, age 62, considering early retirement: If Jim starts his benefits at 62, his monthly benefit would be $1,500, 70% of the total benefit amount he would receive if he waited until his full retirement age of 67. At full retirement age, his monthly benefit would be approximately $2,143. Delaying until age 70 would increase his benefit by 24%, making it about $2,657 monthly due to delayed retirement credits. If Jim expects to live into his late 80s or beyond and has other financial resources, delaying his benefits could provide him with an additional $100,000 or more in lifetime benefits.

Scenario 2: Coordinating Benefits for Married Couples

Karen and Bob, aged 66: Karen's full retirement benefit is $800 per month, while Bob's is $2,500. Karen starts her benefits at 66, but Bob waits until 70 to claim his. This decision increases Bob's monthly benefit to approximately $3,300 due to the 32% increase from delayed retirement credits. This strategy maximizes their monthly income during their joint lifespan. It ensures that Karen will receive a higher survivor benefit of $3,300 per month instead of $2,500 if Bob passes away first, providing greater financial security.

Scenario 3: Divorced and Eligible for Ex-Spousal Benefits

Linda, age 63, divorced: Linda's own Social Security benefit at full retirement age would be $900, but her ex-husband's benefit is $2,400. Since they were married for over 10 years and Linda has not remarried, she qualifies to receive benefits based on her ex-husband's record. At her retirement age of 66, she could receive $1,200 monthly as a spousal benefit, 50% of her ex-husband's full benefit. By claiming this spousal benefit instead of her own at 66, Linda can allow her own benefit to grow. She can then switch to her own benefit at 70, increased to about $1,188 per month due to delayed credits if this amount becomes higher than the spousal benefit. In Linda's case, she should stay with her ex-husband's full benefit.

These detailed scenarios highlight the financial impact of strategic Social Security claiming strategies. By understanding the specific numbers and how different decisions affect overall benefits, retirees can better plan for a financially secure retirement. Each strategy demonstrates how leveraging rules and timing can optimize Social Security benefits to match personal circumstances and financial goals.

Navigating Complex Decisions

Navigating the Social Security landscape requires knowledge and a flair for strategic thinking. In this section, we'll delve into the art of making complex decisions that could significantly impact your financial health in retirement. Let's break down some of these pivotal choices through a break-even analysis and explore how to harmonize Social Security with other retirement income sources.

Life Expectancy and Health Considerations

Your dance with Social Security isn't solo—it partners with your life expectancy and health. If you're in great shape and have a family history of longevity, delaying your benefits could lead to a higher lifetime payout. However, if health issues make your dance card uncertain, starting earlier might be the wiser choice to ensure you maximize your benefits during your retirement.

Coordinating With Other Retirement Income

Once you've mastered your solo, it's time to synchronize your moves with other dancers—your other retirement income sources.

Coordinating Social Security benefits with pensions, IRAs, and other retirement accounts is like choreographing a ballet; every move should be harmonious and enhance the overall performance.

Strategies for Coordination:

- **Pensions and Social Security:** If you have a pension, especially a non-COLA (Cost of Living Adjustment) pension, starting Social Security later might help offset the gradual decrease in your retirement purchasing power.

- **IRAs and Tax Considerations:** Consider the tax implications of withdrawals from retirement accounts. For example, you might use IRA withdrawals to fund your expenses while delaying Social Security to increase your benefits.

- **Flexibility of Withdrawals:** Having multiple income sources allows you to be flexible with your withdrawal strategies, adapting to changes in tax laws, market conditions, and personal needs.

Considerations for a Harmonious Retirement:

- **Tax Planning:** Efficient tax planning ensures unexpected taxes don't trip your dance. Understanding how your Social Security benefits will be taxed with your other retirement income.

- **Market Conditions:** Keep an eye on the market's rhythm. In down years, you might rely more on Social Security and less on withdrawing from investments to avoid selling at a loss.

Navigating these complex decisions with savvy and strategy can dramatically affect your retirement's financial tune, allowing you to live out your retirement years on a high note. This approach isn't just about making smart choices; it's about making choices that resonate with your circumstances, ensuring a retirement filled with financial security and life's joys.

Chapter Exercise: Social Security Planning

Gear up for detective work on your financial future with this engaging exercise designed to map out your potential Social Security claiming strategies. This isn't just about crunching numbers; it's about crafting a plan that aligns with your personal and financial goals.

Objective: This exercise aims to explore different Social Security claiming strategies and understand how each could affect your specific circumstances.

Materials Needed:

1. Access to your Social Security statement (log in or create an account at the Social Security Administration website at SSA.gov)

2. A notebook or digital spreadsheet

3. Calculator (optional since the SSA provides calculators that can do most of the heavy lifting for you)

Steps to Follow:

1. **Gather Your Data:** Log into your Social Security account and download your latest statement. This document will guide you, providing crucial details like your estimated benefits at different ages.

2. **Document Your Scenarios:** Create a simple chart or spreadsheet where you can play around with different ages to start claiming benefits. Include columns for age 62, Full Retirement Age (FRA), and 70. Note the monthly benefit amounts for each age based on the projected benefits listed in your Social Security statement.

3. **Consider Your Variables:** In separate rows, adjust factors that might affect your decision when to claim benefits. These factors include personal health, family longevity, current savings, and other income sources. Use hypothetical scenarios like early retirement due to health issues, working longer than planned, or changes in marital status.

4. **Analysis:** For each scenario, estimate the implications of claiming at different ages. Consider how each decision affects your monthly income, tax situation, and financial security. Use the SSA's online calculators for detailed comparisons and projections.

5. **Reflect on Your Findings:** Review the different outcomes for each strategy. Which option gives you the most financial security? Which strategy aligns best with your lifestyle goals and other retirement plans?

6. **Discuss or Consult:** Discuss your findings with a financial advisor or a knowledgeable friend who can provide feedback on your strategies. Sometimes, an external perspective can highlight considerations you have overlooked.

Outcome: This exercise will familiarize you with the ins and outs of your Social Security benefits and empower you to make informed decisions about when to claim them. By simulating different scenarios, you'll better understand the flexibility and impact of your choices, allowing you to approach your retirement strategy with confidence and clarity.

Your financial future is set to the tune of your life's rhythms. Take the time to ensure the melody is just right, creating a harmonious blend of security and satisfaction in your retirement years.

Making Informed Decisions

As you build your retirement plans, it's essential to remember that the decision on when to begin your Social Security benefits extends beyond mere numbers and calculations.

While the financial benefits of different Social Security claiming strategies are a significant factor, several other considerations should influence your decision:

Health Considerations:

Personal health and expected longevity are some of the most crucial factors. If your health situation suggests a shorter life expectancy, claiming earlier might make more sense. Conversely, excellent health and a family history of longevity could mean delaying benefits to maximize them is a better strategy.

Family Obligations:

Family dynamics, such as being a caregiver or having dependents, can also impact your choice to start taking Social Security. You may need the income sooner to help with family responsibilities or choose to work longer to provide support and delay claiming your benefits.

Personal Goals:

Your vision for retirement and what you hope to accomplish during those years should also guide your decision. If you plan to travel extensively or pursue costly hobbies early in retirement, starting your benefits earlier could help fund those dreams. Alternatively, if your goal is to maximize your financial legacy for heirs, delaying benefits to increase the payout might align better with your objectives.

Consulting With Experts

Navigating Social Security can sometimes feel like interpreting a complex musical score. Just as a conductor leads an orchestra, a financial advisor can guide you through the intricacies of Social Security strategies, ensuring that your choices harmonize with your overall financial plan. Your advisor should consider social security as part of a comprehensive retirement income plan. That plan should take into account:

- **Complexity of Options:** Social Security rules can be intricate. A seasoned professional can provide clarity and insights that help you avoid common pitfalls and capitalize on opportunities you might not know.

- **Personalized Analysis:** Each individual's financial and personal situation is unique. A financial advisor or a Social Security expert can offer tailored advice that considers all aspects of your life, from your health and family situation to your other retirement assets and income sources.

- **Peace of Mind:** Making these decisions can be stressful. Consulting with an expert can provide reassurance that you're making informed choices, giving you confidence in your retirement strategy.

Finding The Right Advisor

Look for professionals with specific experience in retirement planning, especially those familiar with Social Security strategies. Certifications like Certified Financial Planner (CFP), Chartered Financial Consultant (ChFC), or Chartered Retirement Planning Consultant (CRPC) can indicate a high level of expertise.

Consider advisors who work on a fee-only basis or are registered investment advisors who act as fiduciaries to avoid potential conflicts of interest. These advisors don't earn commissions based on their recommended products, which can help ensure their advice is in your best interest.

Making informed decisions about when to start Social Security benefits requires a blend of financial savvy, personal introspection, and sometimes expert guidance. By considering both the numerical analyses and the qualitative aspects of your life, you can orchestrate a retirement strategy that perfectly matches your expectations and needs. Please don't hesitate to seek advice to fine-tune your plans, ensuring that when the curtain rises on your retirement, it's everything you've envisioned and more.

Conclusion: Fine Tuning Your Social Security

As we conclude this chapter on navigating Social Security, it's clear that mastering your benefits is akin to conducting a complex symphony. Each decision point, from timing your benefits to considering your personal and familial circumstances, is critical in how your retirement unfolds.

- **Timing is Crucial:** Deciding when to start receiving Social Security benefits significantly impacts your financial stability. We explored how early, on-time, or delayed claims can affect your monthly income and overall financial health.

- **Holistic Considerations:** Beyond the numbers, factors such as your health, life expectancy, family responsibilities, and personal retirement goals are pivotal in shaping your decision. These elements must harmonize with your financial needs to create a balanced and fulfilling retirement.

- **Expert Guidance:** Given the complexities of Social Security and its profound impact on your retirement, consulting with financial advisors or Social Security experts is recommended. These professionals can provide personalized advice, helping you navigate the intricate details and optimize your benefits based on your unique situation.

- **Stay Informed and Adaptive:** Social Security policies and economic conditions evolve, and so should your strategies. Keep abreast of changes in legislation and economic trends that might affect your benefits, and adjust your plans accordingly.

As you step forward from this chapter, consider yourself more equipped to make informed decisions about your Social Security benefits. Remember, your choices regarding Social Security are not just about securing income but about enhancing the quality and possibilities of your retirement life.

With a solid Social Security strategy, you can focus more on pursuing passions, spending time with loved ones, and exploring new horizons.

Social Security is a vital part of your retirement ensemble. Still, your proactive engagement with these benefits will make your retirement years resonate with security and satisfaction. Embrace this journey with enthusiasm and confidence, knowing you are well-prepared to make the most of the opportunities.

Chapter 9

Understanding Pensions

"In retirement, your financial independence is your greatest asset—nurture it."

As we dive into pensions, it's important to note that not everyone will have a pension plan waiting for them in retirement. If you're among those without a pension, skip this chapter and move on to other topics more relevant to your retirement planning. For those with access to a pension, understanding how it functions can significantly impact your financial security in your golden years.

Defined Benefit vs Defined Contribution Plans

Understanding the mechanics and implications of different types of pension plans is crucial for effective retirement planning. Let's delve deeper into how defined benefit and contribution plans work, their advantages, and the challenges they present.

Defined Benefit Plans

How They Work: Defined benefit plans are structured around a formula that usually includes factors like your salary and length of employment. Typically, the formula is 1.5% of your average salary for the last three years of employment multiplied by the number of years you worked. This setup ensures that the benefit you receive is predictable and insulated from market fluctuations.

Advantages:

- **Security and Predictability:** The foremost advantage of defined benefit plans is their security. Retirees receive a fixed monthly amount, which makes budgeting straightforward and reliable.

- **Less Personal Risk Management:** Since the payouts are not directly tied to the market's performance, retirees with defined benefit plans don't need to worry about investment risks as they approach retirement.

Challenges:

- **Decreasing Prevalence:** Over recent decades, the availability of defined benefit plans has declined as employers shift toward less costly retirement options, such as defined contribution plans.

- **Funding Issues:** Many defined benefit plans are underfunded, meaning their liabilities exceed their assets, which can pose risks to the security of promised benefits. Additionally, managing these funds can impact their ability to meet long-term obligations to retirees.

Defined Contribution Plans

In contrast to defined benefit plans, defined contribution plans are based on contributions made by employees and employers into individual accounts, which are then invested. The final benefit depends on the performance of these investments. Standard defined contribution plans include 401(k)s and 403(b)s, where employees can influence their investment choices among stocks, bonds, and mutual funds.

Advantages:

- **Potential for Higher Returns:** Contributions invested in the market have the potential for higher returns compared to the typically conservative investment strategies of defined benefit plans.

- **Flexibility and Control:** Employees have more control over their investments, which can be adjusted based on personal risk tolerance and market conditions. This control allows for tailored retirement strategies that can maximize growth.

Challenges:

- **Market Risk:** The downside of potential higher returns is the exposure to market volatility. Poor investment performance can significantly impact the retirement benefits available, placing more pressure on individuals to manage their investments wisely.

- **Responsibility on Individuals:** The burden of ensuring adequate retirement funds lies heavily on the individual. This requires a proactive approach to retirement planning and more significant financial literacy to manage investments effectively.

Both defined benefit and contribution plans have distinct roles, benefits, and drawbacks in retirement planning. Understanding these will help you navigate your options and strategies for a secure and fulfilling retirement. Whether your employer offers one or both, knowing how to optimize your benefits within these plans can significantly impact your financial security in your golden years.

The Decline Of Traditional Pension Plans

In the landscape of retirement options, traditional pension plans, or defined benefit plans, once stood as towering oaks, offering robust shelter against financial storms in retirement. Let's explore the journey of these plans, from their peak to their gradual decline, and understand what this means for today's retirees.

Back then, traditional pensions were the gold standard of retirement security. They offered a clear promise: work for a company for many years, and you'll be rewarded with a steady income in retirement, like a faithful old workhorse that keeps plowing the field long after its prime.

How They Worked:

- **Employer Commitment:** Employers were responsible for funding and managing large pools of assets to ensure that every retiree received their promised benefits, regardless of market conditions. This arrangement was less about individual gains and more about collective security.

- **Lifetime Assurance:** For employees, this meant a predictable and secure income waiting at the end of a long career, a proper "set it and forget it" model where retirement planning required less personal oversight.

However, traditional pensions, such as vinyl records and drive-in theaters, have seen their popularity wane over the decades. Several factors contributed to this shift:

Economic Shifts:

As the global economy evolved, the stability and predictability of long-term investments became more challenging to maintain. Increased longevity also meant that companies were on the hook for more extended retirement payouts, significantly raising the cost of keeping pension plans.

Corporate Cost-Cutting:

With the rise of shareholder value as a corporate mantra, companies began to see defined benefit plans as expensive relics. The financial burden of funding these plans, especially during economic downturns, led many companies to seek more cost-effective alternatives.

Rise of Defined Contribution Plans:

The introduction and rise of defined contribution plans, such as 401(k)s, marked a significant shift in retirement planning. These plans transferred the risk and responsibility from the employer to the employee, aligning with a broader move towards individualism in financial planning. Employees now had the freedom to grow their retirement savings but also bore the brunt of the risks.

Navigating The World Without A Traditional Pension

For many of today's workers, the reality is that they will not have access to a traditional pension plan. This shift necessitates a more proactive approach to retirement planning:

Self-Education:

With the safety net of a defined benefit plan, individuals can become more financially literate, understanding how to save, invest, and plan for their retirement.

Diversified Planning:

It's crucial to put only some of your eggs in one basket. Diversifying your retirement savings across various accounts, including IRAs, 401(k)s, and other investment vehicles, becomes paramount in ensuring financial security.

Seeking Stability:

In a world without the guaranteed income from traditional pensions, finding other stable income sources, such as Social Security or annuities, becomes even more critical.

As we reflect on the evolution of retirement plans, it's clear that the landscape has shifted dramatically. The decline of traditional pensions has left a gap that requires both adaptability and a proactive approach to retirement planning. As nostalgic as one might be for the simplicity and security of the past, looking forward and planning wisely with the available tools is the key to a secure and rewarding retirement.

Pensions and Retirement Security

As we navigate the evolving world of retirement planning, integrating pensions into your broader retirement strategy remains crucial for those with them. This section explores how to weave pension benefits into your retirement tapestry, ensuring that every financial thread strengthens your overall security.

Harmonizing Various Income Streams:

- **Complementing Social Security:** Pensions can serve as a reliable base layer of income, complementing Social Security. For example, suppose your pension covers your basic living expenses. In that case, you may delay Social Security benefits to maximize your payout, thus enhancing your financial stability in later retirement.

- **Balancing with Personal Savings:** If you have a pension and personal savings or investments, consider balancing withdrawals to maintain a steady income flow while keeping taxes and investment risks in check. This might mean tapping into personal savings sparingly in early retirement to let them grow, relying more heavily on pension payouts during this period.

Creating a Seamless Financial Blend:

Use tools like income projection calculators to visualize how your pension interacts with other income sources year by year. This will help you see where shortfalls or surpluses might be, allowing you to adjust accordingly.

When receiving your pension benefits, you generally have a few choices, each with its own considerations. Understanding these options can help you make decisions that best fit your financial needs and retirement goals.

Lump Sum vs. Annuity Payments:

There are typically two payment options available to you when you elect to take your pension: Lump Sum or Annuity. Choosing a lump sum payout means receiving the entire value of your pension in one go. This option provides flexibility and control over your funds, allowing you to invest or use them as you see fit. However, managing a large sum requires financial savvy to ensure it lasts throughout retirement and doesn't bring hefty tax burdens all at once.

Opting for annuity payments converts your pension into a regular, guaranteed income stream for Life or a specified term. This choice mirrors the reliability of traditional pensions. Knowing you have a steady income each month can provide peace of mind. One thing to consider is whether to choose Life only or survivor benefits. If you have a spouse or significant other who can qualify as a beneficiary on the plan if you choose Life only when you are gone, so is the income stream, leaving your partner with no income from the pension.

This choice is often the biggest regret I see from clients who did not work with me before choosing their pension options. The more significant payment from the Life only option seems better when they are retired and healthy. Later in Life, when they may be experiencing severe health issues, they see the problem of not having a pension for their partner once they are gone if they have not managed their other funds well. If you are a DIY'er and only engage a Financial Planner once, ensure you do it before selecting your pension option. You only get one chance to do it right, so get help to model the potential options.

Factors to Consider:

- **Tax Implications:** Understand how your choice affects your tax situation. Annuity payments might keep you in a lower tax bracket compared to taking a large lump sum.

- **Investment Opportunities:** If you opt for a lump sum, consider your ability to manage and invest that money. While it offers growth potential, it also comes with investment risks.

- **Longevity Risk:** Annuity payments can protect against the risk of outliving your savings, a crucial consideration if longevity runs in your family.

Making the Decision:

Consider your overall health, life expectancy, financial understanding, and the needs of any dependents. Consulting with a financial advisor can provide personalized insights based on these factors.

Chapter Exercise: Pension Plan Analysis

Suppose you're one of the fortunate individuals with a pension plan. In that case, understanding the nuances of your specific plan is essential for maximizing your retirement benefits. This exercise will guide you through a detailed pension plan analysis, helping you grasp its advantages and limitations.

Objective

This exercise aims to clearly understand your pension plan's features, how it fits into your overall retirement strategy, and how to make informed decisions based on its benefits and potential drawbacks.

Materials Needed

- Your pension plan documents

- A recent pension statement (if available)

- Calculator

- Notebook or spreadsheet software

Steps to Follow

1. **Gather Your Documents:**

- Collect all relevant documents related to your pension plan. These include your initial plan agreement, annual statements, and any updates you've received.

- If you need these documents, you can obtain them by contacting your employer's human resources department or the pension plan administrator.

1. **Understand Your Plan Type:**

- Determine whether you have a defined benefit or a defined contribution plan. Review this chapter's introduction and earlier sections for a refresher on the differences.

1. **Analyze Plan Benefits:**

Look for the formula used to calculate your benefits. Note your salary, years of service, and any other variables that affect the calculation.

2. **Review Payout Options:**

Identify your plan's different payout options, such as lump sum, life annuity, or joint and survivor annuity. Note the conditions and implications of each option.

3. **Evaluate Plan Limitations and Risks:**

- Consider any potential risks associated with your plan, such as underfunding concerns for defined benefit plans or investment risks for defined contribution plans.

- Look for any clauses about plan changes, including benefit adjustments or plan termination.

4. Integrate with Other Retirement Income:

- Using a spreadsheet, map out how your pension income will work alongside other retirement income sources like Social Security and personal savings. Estimate how these sources together will cover your anticipated retirement expenses.

5. Reflect and Plan Next Steps:

- Reflect on how secure and adequate your pension benefits are within your retirement income plan.

- Based on the analysis, consider whether you need to increase your personal savings or adjust your retirement strategies.

6. Consult a Professional (Optional but recommended):

- Given the complexity of some pension plans, especially in the context of an entire retirement strategy, consulting with a financial advisor can provide additional clarity and personalized advice.

Outcome

By the end of this exercise, you should have a comprehensive understanding of how your pension plan works, its role within your broader retirement portfolio, and any actions you might need to take to optimize your financial readiness for retirement. This analysis empowers you with knowledge and ensures you are better prepared to make informed decisions that enhance your financial security during retirement.

Wrap-Up: Securing Your Retirement With A Pension

As we wrap up this chapter on understanding pensions, it's clear that these retirement plans, whether defined benefit or defined contribution, play a pivotal role in shaping your financial landscape in retirement. Proper management and a deep understanding of your pension plan can significantly enhance your financial stability and comfort during your golden years.

Pensions are more than just financial instruments; they are bridges to a secure and worry-free retirement. Understanding the nuances of your pension—how it works, what benefits it offers, and the limitations it might have—is crucial. Whether you have a defined benefit plan that promises a fixed payout or a defined contribution plan that grows based on market investments, each type has unique characteristics that can impact your retirement: **Defined Benefit Plans** provide predictable, steady income but require awareness of the plan's funding and stability.

By understanding these differences and how each plan fits into your overall retirement strategy, you can make more informed decisions that ensure a comfortable retirement.

To truly secure your retirement, it is essential not to be passive about your pension. Here are a few steps to take a proactive approach to managing your pension benefits:

- **Stay Informed:** Keep up-to-date with any changes to your pension plan and broader changes in pension legislation that might affect your benefits.

- **Consult with Professionals:** Consider seeking advice from financial professionals who can offer personalized insights into utilizing your pension with other retirement funds. They can help craft a strategy that maximizes your retirement income while minimizing risks.

- **Regular Reviews:** Make it a habit to regularly review your retirement strategy to ensure that your pension continues to meet your needs. As your financial situation or the economic environment changes, you may need to adjust your plans.

Be sure to start understanding and managing your pension before retirement. Take the reins by reviewing your current pension plan details, assessing how they fit into your broader retirement aspirations, and adjusting your strategies as necessary. Remember, your decisions today will shape your financial well-being in retirement.

Armed with the knowledge from this chapter, you are better prepared to navigate the complexities of pensions and ensure that this critical component of your retirement planning is aligned with your long-term financial goals. So, dive into your pension details, schedule a consultation with a retirement planner, and take active steps toward securing a prosperous and stable retirement.

Chapter 10

Demystifying Income Annuities

"Longevity is both a gift and a challenge—plan to live long, and live well."

This is likely the most controversial chapter in the book. The financial media and investment gurus love to hate annuities. You have to realize that most of these famous people are paid by selling you books and programs, and most of them have not actually sat down with a real client in years or possibly ever. They are wonderful theorists and entertaining personalities, but in most cases, they have no actual facts to back up their claims of the horrors of these products.

Now, let me take the other side of this argument. Annuities are wildly oversold by the financial industry, specifically by advisors who are only insurance and not securities licensed. If someone recommends that you take your entire retirement savings or is pressuring you with scare tactics (in the guise of a FREE steak dinner), I would get up and walk away immediately. Enough said on that.

Annuities are financial products designed to offer retirees a steady income stream, typically for life. By converting a lump sum into regular payments, annuities can provide a reliable foundation for retirement, much like traditional pensions. However, unlike pensions, which are generally employer-funded, annuities are personal contracts that you purchase from an insurance company.

Understanding Immediate Annuities

In this section, we'll explore immediate annuities in their various forms, including deferred and variable annuities. Each type has distinct features and benefits tailored to different retirement planning needs.

Immediate annuities are often likened to jumping into a swimming pool—the impact is immediate and designed to last. You invest a lump sum with an insurance company when you purchase an immediate annuity. In return, you start receiving payments almost immediately. These payments can continue for the duration of your life or a set period, depending on your chosen terms.

Payout Options:

- **Life-Only:** This option typically offers the highest monthly payment but ceases upon the annuitant's death. It's straightforward: payments for life, no residual benefit for heirs.

- **Life with Term Certain:** Combines lifetime payments with a guaranteed payout period (e.g., 10, 20 years). If you pass away before the end of the Term, your beneficiaries receive the remaining payments.

- **Joint Life:** Ideal for couples, this option continues payments as long as either spouse lives, ensuring that the surviving spouse continues to receive income.

These choices reflect a trade-off between maximizing income and providing for heirs, requiring careful consideration based on your family situation and financial goals.

Deferred Income Annuities

While immediate annuities start paying out shortly after investment, deferred income annuities (DIAs) are the slow cookers of the annuity world—they take time to mature but promise comforting financial warmth later in retirement.

Deferred income annuities are a strategic choice for those who have covered their near-term retirement expenses but want to ensure they keep their resources.

In our practice, we typically use DIAs and other similar vehicles for preplanning (let's say 5-7 years out from retirement) so that we can take some of your risk-oriented money off the table and lock down those first few years of retirement income from market corrections.

Variable Annuities

Variable annuities offer a different kind of engagement, akin to sailing in open waters where the winds of market performance can significantly influence your journey. With variable annuities, your payments are tied to the performance of investment options you select, such as mutual funds.

Potential for Higher Returns:

- The appeal of variable annuities lies in their potential for higher returns. If the chosen investments perform well, you could see substantial growth in your annuity value and, subsequently, higher income payouts.

- **Customization:** You can tailor your investment choices based on your risk tolerance and financial goals, adjusting your portfolio as market conditions change.

Higher Risk:

- However, the flip side is higher risk. Investment performance can lead to higher payouts, which might not keep pace with inflation or meet your income needs.

Variable annuities require a more active management approach and understanding of market dynamics. This makes them suitable for more financially savvy retirees or those working closely with a financial advisor.

Immediate, deferred, and variable annuities serve unique roles in retirement planning, catering to different needs, from immediate income provision to long-term security with growth potential. As you consider incorporating annuities into your retirement plan, weigh their features and benefits against your personal circumstances and financial objectives. Remember, the correct type of annuity can enhance your retirement security, providing peace of mind that your financial needs will be met, come what may.

Debunking Myths and Understanding Realities

Annuities are often surrounded by misconceptions that can deter individuals from considering them viable retirement options. In this section, we'll clear the fog around common myths and provide a balanced perspective on the benefits and drawbacks of incorporating annuities into your retirement strategy.

Common Myths

Myth 1: Annuities Come with Prohibitive High Fees

- **Reality:** While it's true that some annuities, especially variable annuities, can have higher fees, not all annuities are created equal. Fixed annuities and immediate annuities often have lower fees. It's crucial to shop around and understand the fee structure of any annuity before purchasing. Working with an advisor who does holistic planning can be a huge benefit instead of working with someone who only sells insurance.

Myth 2: You Lose Control Over Your Money

- **Reality:** Some believe that you lose control over those funds once you purchase an annuity. While annuities involve committing a lump sum or series of payments, many products offer riders or features that allow for some liquidity, emergency withdrawals, or even legacy options for beneficiaries.

Myth 3: Annuities are Too Complex

- **Reality:** Annuities can be complex but don't have to be overwhelming. With the correct information and guidance, you can find an understandable annuity product that fits well with your financial goals. Once again, Financial Advisors can be crucial in demystifying the terms and conditions.

Benefits of Annuities

Incorporating annuities into your retirement plan can offer several significant benefits:

- **Guaranteed Income Stream:** Perhaps annuities' most appealing feature is their ability to provide a guaranteed income for life, which can be a cornerstone of a secure retirement strategy.

- **Protection Against Longevity Risk:** Annuities can protect against the risk of outliving your savings, a concern for many as life expectancies increase.

- **Tax Advantages:** Annuities provide tax-deferred growth, which means you will only pay taxes on the earnings once you withdraw them, potentially reducing your tax burden during the accumulation phase.

Drawbacks of Annuities

However, annuities are not without their potential drawbacks, which include:

- **Inflexibility:** Once you commit to an annuity, particularly with immediate annuities, you may have limited access to your funds, making it crucial to ensure you have other liquid assets for unexpected needs.

- **Fees and Expenses:** Certain types of annuities, especially variable annuities, can have high fees that can reduce your returns. It's essential to understand all the costs involved before making a decision.

- **Impact of Inflation:** One major concern for fixed annuities is inflation, which can diminish the purchasing power of fixed payments over time. Some annuities offer inflation protection, but this typically comes at the cost of a lower starting payment.

Annuities can play a vital role in a well-rounded retirement plan, offering predictable income and peace of mind. However, like any investment product, they are not one-size-fits-all. Understanding annuities' myths and realities will empower you to make decisions that align with your retirement goals and financial situation. Assess the benefits and weigh them against the drawbacks, consult with financial professionals, and consider how an annuity might fit into your broader financial landscape. By doing so, you can use annuities as a financial tool and a strategic asset in achieving a secure and fulfilling retirement.

Evaluating And Choosing Annuities

Choosing the right annuity is akin to selecting the perfect instrument to complement a well-orchestrated symphony—each choice resonates through your financial future. This section will guide you through assessing the suitability of an annuity for your retirement strategy and offer insights on picking the best type for your individual needs.

Assessing Suitability

When considering an annuity, it's crucial to tune into your financial situation and long-term goals. Here's how to evaluate whether an annuity fits into your retirement ensemble:

- **Financial Needs:** Assess your expected retirement expenses and determine how much you want to be guaranteed by an annuity. Consider whether you need immediate income or if you can delay payments to increase benefits.

- **Risk Tolerance:** Understand your comfort level with risk, especially considering variable annuities. Are you looking for a stable, predictable income, or will you accept some market risk for potentially higher returns?

- **Other Income Sources:** Consider how an annuity fits with other income sources like Social Security, pensions, or investments. Annuities can fill gaps, ensuring that essential expenses are always covered.

- **Overall Financial Goals:** Reflect on how an annuity supports your financial goals. Are you primarily concerned with preserving capital or aiming for growth and leaving a legacy?

Choosing The Right Annuity

Selecting the right annuity involves more than identifying your needs—it involves finding a product that aligns with those needs while offering the best terms and security.

- **Type of Annuity:** Decide between immediate, deferred, fixed, variable, or indexed annuities based on when you need income and how you want to manage investment risk.

- **Fees and Expenses:** Look for transparent pricing and reasonable costs. Variable annuities, in particular, can have layers of fees that may impact the net benefit.

- **Insurer Stability and Ratings:** Choose a financially stable insurance company. Check ratings through agencies like A.M. Best, Fitch, Moody's, or Standard & Poor's to gauge the insurer's ability to meet financial commitments.

- **Payout Options and Riders:** Consider the flexibility of payout options and the availability of riders that can tailor the annuity to your needs. Everyday riders include cost-of-living adjustments, death benefits, and emergency withdrawal features.

Exercise: Annuity Evaluation

Put theory into practice with this hands-on exercise designed to help you evaluate potential annuity products based on your retirement strategy.

Materials Needed:

- A list of available annuity products

- A financial calculator

- Access to insurer ratings

Steps:

- **List Your Requirements:** Write down your specific needs from an annuity, including income start date, desired payout, and critical features like inflation protection.

- **Research Products:** Use your requirements to identify several annuity products that match your criteria. Note their fees, terms, and insurer ratings.

- **Compare Features:** Create a comparison chart that includes your top annuity choices. Evaluate each based on its suitability for your needs, costs, and the insurer's financial strength.

- **Scenario Analysis:** For each annuity option, consider different scenarios, such as changes in market conditions or personal circumstances. How would each product perform?

- **Make a Decision:** Based on your comparison and scenarios, determine which annuity offers the best balance of security, cost, and flexibility to meet your retirement goals.

Engaging in a thorough evaluation and selection process will empower you to choose an annuity that harmonizes perfectly with your retirement plans. Remember, the goal is not just to find an annuity but the right one for your unique symphony of retirement needs. This proactive approach ensures that your retirement is as lyrical and worry-free as possible when the time comes.

Final Thoughts: The Role of Income Annuities In Retirement

Income annuities can be likened to the foundation of a house, providing the stability that allows you to build upwards confidently. In the structure of retirement planning, they ensure that no matter how the financial markets perform or how long you live, you have a steady stream of income to cover essential expenses. This peace of mind is invaluable, as it frees you to enjoy your retirement fully without constant worry over finances.

- **Guaranteed Income:** This is the most compelling aspect of annuities. The assurance of a guaranteed payout eliminates the fear of outliving your savings, making it easier to plan for a secure and enjoyable future.

- **Diversification:** While other retirement income sources like stocks, bonds, and rental properties can fluctuate with market conditions, annuities provide a steady, predictable income that complements these more variable sources. This balance is critical to creating a comprehensive retirement plan to weather different economic climates.

While this chapter has provided a broad overview of what annuities can offer, every individual's financial situation is unique. Therefore, it's crucial to delve deeper into how annuities might fit into your specific retirement plan:

- **Conduct Further Research:** Research different types of annuities and their providers. Look into the specifics of each product, such as fees, payout options, and additional riders that might benefit you.

- **Consult with a Financial Advisor:** An expert can offer personalized advice tailored to your financial circumstances and retirement goals. They can help you understand the complex aspects of annuities and how to integrate them effectively with your other retirement income sources.

- **Evaluate Your Retirement Goals:** Regularly reassess your retirement strategy to ensure it remains aligned with your goals. As your needs and the economic environment evolve, so should your plan.

Incorporating annuities into your retirement planning isn't just about securing income—it's about crafting a retirement lifestyle rich in possibility and devoid of financial anxiety. By ensuring a portion of your income is guaranteed, you open up a world where retirement is not just a time of life but a time for living.

Take the initiative to understand how annuities can enhance your financial security and consult with professionals to tailor a plan that fits your vision of a perfect retirement. With the proper planning and tools at your disposal, you can look forward to a future that is as stable as it is satisfying.

Chapter 11

Building Your Essential Income Plan

"Your essential income pool should be your safety net, covering all non-negotiable expenses."

As we begin crafting your essential income plan, it's crucial to understand the role and importance of essential income in your retirement strategy. Essential income is the portion of your retirement income earmarked for non-negotiable living expenses—those costs you must cover to maintain a basic, comfortable standard of living.

What is Essential Income?

Essential income covers the bedrock expenses in your life. This is typically not going to be the "Fun Stuff" but the things that you cannot live life without. Some people may argue that cable and Netflix are necessary and essential expenses, but typically, the main ones are:

- **Housing:** Whether it's mortgage payments, rent, or maintenance fees, having a secure place to call home is paramount.

- **Food:** Regular, nutritious meals are a fundamental need.

- **Healthcare:** From routine doctor visits to unexpected medical needs, healthcare costs can be significant as you age.

- **Basic Utilities:** Electricity, water, heating, and other utilities are indispensable for a safe and comfortable home environment.

This income stream should be as reliable and predictable as the sunrise because these are not expenses you can defer or eliminate. They are constant and enduring, much like the foundation of a house that supports everything built upon it.

The security of knowing that your essential needs are met without fail is more than just comforting; it's empowering. Here's why securing this part of your income is critical:

- **Financial Stability:** By reliably covering essential expenses, you're safeguarded against the unpredictability of other income sources, such as investments that might fluctuate with market conditions.

- **Peace of Mind:** There'sKnowing you can afford to live comfortably brings invaluable peace. This tranquility allows you to enjoy other aspects of retirement more fully without the nagging worry of financial instability.

- **Freedom to Enjoy Retirement:** Once the essentials are secured, any additional income can be used for the more enjoyable aspects of retirement, such as travel, hobbies, or spoiling the grandchildren. This setup ensures that your retirement is not just endured but enjoyed.

The following sections will explore how to strategically build and fortify this essential income stream, examining various sources like Social Security, pensions, annuities, and other reliable income vehicles. We'll also explore integrating these sources effectively to create a robust financial foundation supporting your retirement dreams. The goal is to construct a plan so solid that even in the face of economic storms, your essential needs remain unshaken.

Identifying Essential Expenses

As we reviewed before, creating a robust essential income plan begins with clearly understanding your necessary expenses. You must meet these non-negotiable expenses to maintain a basic, comfortable standard of living throughout retirement.

Categorizing Your Expenses:

- **Housing:** This includes your mortgage or rent, property taxes, homeowners' insurance, and essential maintenance.

- **Utilities:** Regular bills such as electricity, water, gas, and essential telecommunications services (phone, internet) fall into this category.

- **Food:** Regular grocery bills and necessary dietary needs are considered essential.

- **Healthcare:** Monthly premiums for health insurance, expected out-of-pocket costs, regular medications, and any known medical procedures should be included.

- **Transportation:** Basic transportation costs like fuel, insurance, regular maintenance, and possibly public transit fares are essential, especially if you need a vehicle for doctor appointments or grocery shopping.

Reviewing your current spending to accurately categorize and understand your essential expenses is crucial. Review bank statements, bills, and receipts from the past year to ensure all recurring costs are accounted for.

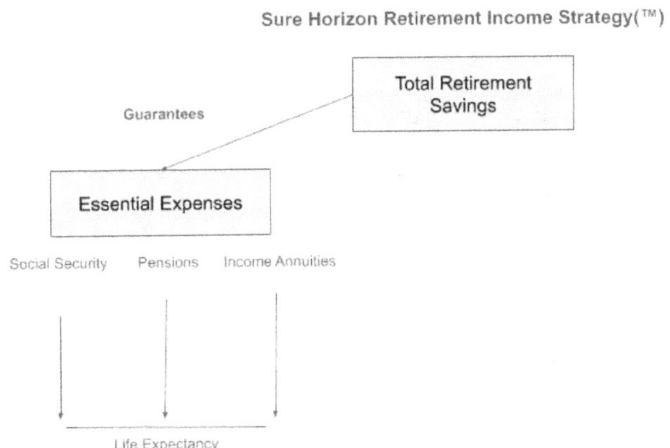

Projecting Future Costs

Understanding your current essential expenses is just the start. It would help if you also considered how these costs might increase over time, mainly due to inflation and changes in your circumstances.

Accounting for Inflation:

- **General Inflation:** The general cost of living will likely increase over time. A rule of thumb is to plan for an annual inflation rate of 2-3%, which can compound significantly over a long retirement.

- **Sector-Specific Inflation:** Certain costs, like healthcare, tend to increase at a rate higher than general inflation. Historical data can be helpful, and planning for healthcare inflation rates of 4-6% per year may be prudent.

Methods to Estimate Future Costs:

- **Use Historical Averages:** To guide your estimates, look at the historical inflation rates over the past 20-30 years.

- **Financial Calculators:** Use online calculators that factor in inflation to project your future expenses. These tools can adjust your current expenses to future values using various inflation rates.

- **Consult with Professionals:** Financial advisors can provide valuable insights and projections based on current economic trends and personal financial situations. For example, the software we use to build financial plans for our clients not only builds in inflation but can also project what taxes will look like.

Exercise: Estimating Essential Retirement Expenses

This exercise will help you visualize and plan for your future essential expenses, ensuring you have a realistic and comprehensive understanding as you enter retirement.

> We have put together a FREE Toolkit that you can use to go through the exercises in this book. The workbook takes you through completing your Sure Horizon Retirement Income Plan™. You can download your FREE copy at www.sure-horizonretirement.com/toolkit

Steps:

- **List Current Essential Expenses:** Start with a detailed list of your monthly or annual expenses.

- **Apply Inflation Rates:** Using a simple spreadsheet, apply estimated inflation rates to these expenses for each year of your expected retirement.

- **Consider Changes in Needs:** Adjust for changes in your lifestyle that might affect these costs, such as paying off a mortgage, changes in medical needs, or relocating to a different area with different living costs.

- **Review Annually:** Make it a habit to review and adjust these projections annually based on real-world changes in costs and personal circumstances.

By systematically assessing and projecting your essential expenses, you'll be better equipped to ensure that your retirement income plan is realistic and sufficient to cover your needs. This careful planning allows you to approach retirement confidently, knowing that your fundamental financial needs are securely managed.

Mapping Income to Expenses

To ensure a stable and comfortable retirement, aligning your guaranteed income sources with your essential expenses is crucial. This alignment ensures that your basic needs are met without fail, providing financial stability and peace of mind. It is important to remember that you typically have monthly expenses like housing and utilities. Still, you may also have once-a-year expenses like homeowners insurance, possibly car insurance, and real estate taxes, which may be "lumpy" expenses in your budget. You want to ensure that you account for those in your monthly cash flow and save that money in a savings account until needed. That will ensure you don't have cash flow issues throughout the year.

Steps to Align Income with Expenses:

- **List Guaranteed Income Sources:** List all your guaranteed income sources, such as Social Security, pensions, and income annuities. Note their monthly or annual payout amounts.

- **Match Income to Monthly and Annual Expenses:** Using a detailed budget, align your income sources with your expenses. For instance, set your Social Security to cover utilities and groceries, your pension for housing, and annuities for healthcare costs.

- **Adjust for Timing:** Ensure that the timing of your income matches your expense needs. Some costs, like property taxes or insurance premiums, may be annual and require planning to ensure funds are available when needed.

Optimize Your Social Security

As discussed in Chapter 7, you need a strategy for Social Security. Social security is often the cornerstone of retirement planning, and maximizing its benefits can significantly enhance your financial well-being in retirement.

Strategies for Maximizing Benefits:

- **Delay Benefits:** Delaying the start of your Social Security benefits can increase your monthly payout. This may be beneficial if you can afford to wait, especially if you expect a longer-than-average lifespan. Consider using assets from your 401k or other savings early on in your plan to delay Social for as long as possible.

- **Consider Health and Longevity:** Start benefits earlier if you have health issues or a shorter family longevity history. This may allow you to maximize your benefits.

- **Coordinate with Your Spouse:** If married, consider strategies such as claiming one spouse's benefits early while delaying the other's for maximum overall benefit. This often works well if one spouse makes significantly more than the other. Lower-earning spouses can claim benefits when they reach Full Retirement Age (FRA). In contrast, the higher-earning spouse can claim theirs at age 70, locking in the much larger check and a more extensive base for COLA adjustments over time.

Leveraging Pensions

As discussed in Chapter 8, a pension is a significant foundation for your Retirement Income Plan. Pensions provide a reliable income stream, and making the most of them is critical to a secure retirement.

Pension Payout Options:

- **Lump Sum vs. Regular Payments:** Weigh the benefits of receiving a lump sum against the reliability of regular annuity payments. While a lump sum offers flexibility and investment potential, regular payments provide a guaranteed income not subject to market fluctuations.

- **Consider Your Overall Financial Picture:** If you have substantial savings or other income sources, you might opt for the lump sum to invest or manage as part of a broader financial strategy. Otherwise, regular payments offer more security.

As I wrote in the pension chapter, one of the biggest regrets I experience from clients regarding pensions is when they choose a Life Income option instead of a survivor benefit. This leaves your spouse or significant other without that pension income when you are gone.

A strategy called **Pension Maximization** elects to use the Life Option of your pension. When doing pension maximization, you must analyze the difference between the life Only and your pension's 100% survivor option. Suppose the monthly income difference is enough between the two. In that case, you may be able to purchase a permanent life insurance policy that will provide enough death benefits to replace the lost income after your death. We regularly do this for our clients as they make these decisions. I suggest finding someone who understands these calculations to help you look at all the variables. The good thing is that there is no gray area. It is just math; it either works or doesn't.

Incorporating Income Annuities

Chapter 9 discussed how annuities can play a critical role in bridging gaps between your guaranteed income and essential expenses. As you continue to build your essential income plan, consider injecting an income annuity into the mix if there is a gap.

Using Annuities Effectively:

- **Immediate Annuities are ideal** for providing a steady income stream right after retirement. They can be particularly useful if there's a gap before other retirement benefits, like Social Security, kick in.

- **Deferred Income Annuities:** These are useful for locking in money that you have committed to essential income in a few years down the road.

- **Choose the Right Type for Your Needs:** A combination of immediate and deferred annuities might be optimal depending on your financial situation. Assess your cash flow needs and potential expenses to determine the best mix.

Integrating guaranteed income sources effectively requires a comprehensive understanding of your income streams and spending needs. By strategically mapping out how each source of income will cover specific expenses, you can ensure a smooth and secure financial flow throughout retirement. Remember, each decision you make about Social Security, pensions, and annuities should fit your current financial landscape and provide guarantees to cover future changes in your expenses and income needs.

The Role Of Professional Advice

Balancing multiple income sources and predicting long-term needs can be daunting when securing your financial future through retirement. This is where the expertise of a financial advisor becomes invaluable. A professional can tailor your essential income plan to fit your unique circumstances, providing a level of customization that isn't just comforting—it's financially prudent.

Advantages of Consulting a Financial Advisor:

- **Expert Insights:** Financial advisors bring a depth of knowledge about investment strategies, tax implications, and retirement planning that is difficult to match.

- **Holistic Approach:** They look at the entire picture of your financial health, including assets, liabilities, income streams, and personal goals, to create a balanced plan that aligns with your retirement objectives.

- **Complex Financial Situations:** For those with more complicated financial backgrounds—such as owning multiple investment properties, having a mixed portfolio of stocks and bonds, or dealing with inheritance issues—a financial advisor can navigate the intricacies and optimize your financial strategy.

Our firm takes on a few clients per month. If you want to work with us to develop your retirement income plan, you can visit this website to schedule an intro call. <Insert Scheduling URL Here>.

Chapter Exercise: Gap Analysis

In this exercise, we'll guide you through a detailed analysis to identify potential gaps between your projected essential expenses and your expected guaranteed income in retirement. Identifying these gaps early allows you to proactively address them, ensuring a stable and secure financial future.

Objectives

- Understand the full scope of your essential expenses.

- Align these expenses with your guaranteed income sources.

- Identify any shortfalls and explore solutions to address these gaps.

Materials Needed

- A list of your expected retirement income sources (Social Security, pensions, annuities, etc.)

- Detailed monthly or annual budget of your essential expenses

- Calculator

- Notebook or spreadsheet for calculations

Steps to Conduct a Gap Analysis

1. List Your Guaranteed Income Sources:

- Write down all your guaranteed income sources and their monthly or annual amounts. This could include Social Security payments, pension benefits, and income from annuities.

2. Detail Your Essential Expenses:

- Create a comprehensive list of your monthly or annual essential expenses, including housing, food, healthcare, and utilities.

3. Calculate Total Income and Expenses:

- Sum up your total guaranteed income and your total essential expenses. Use a spreadsheet for easy calculations and adjustments.

4. Identify Any Shortfalls:

- Subtract your total essential expenses from your total guaranteed income. A positive number means you have surplus income; a negative number indicates a gap.

5. Addressing the Gaps:

- If you discover a shortfall, consider the following strategies:

- **Increase Income:** Explore options for additional annuities, particularly deferred income annuities that can provide higher payouts later in retirement.

- **Adjust Living Standards:** Review your essential expenses to identify areas where adjustments can be made without significantly impacting your lifestyle.

- **Investment Income:** Consider ways to generate additional income through safe investments or downsizing assets.

6. Plan for Inflation:

- Adjust your calculations for future inflation, especially healthcare and housing costs, to ensure your gap analysis remains relevant.

7. Review Annually:

- Make it a habit to perform this gap analysis annually or whenever there's a significant change in your income or expenses. This will help you stay on top of your financial situation and adjust as needed.

Tips for Success

- **Be Conservative in Estimates:** Err on the side of caution when estimating expenses and inflation. Planning for higher expenses and being pleasantly surprised is better than finding yourself short on funds.

- **Consult with a Financial Advisor:** For complex situations or significant shortfalls, consulting with a professional can provide tailored advice and innovative solutions.

Performing a gap analysis is a crucial exercise in retirement planning. It lets you visualize your financial future clearly and take necessary actions to ensure your golden years are as secure and enjoyable as possible. Regularly updating this analysis allows you to adapt to changes in your financial landscape and maintain peace of mind, knowing that your essential needs will always be met.

If you would like to see me walk through all the steps of creating a Sure Horizon Retirement Income Strategy™ (if you haven't already), you can access the recording here at www.SureHorizonRetirement.com/masterclass

Wrap-Up: Reinforcing Security With A Well-Structured Essential Income Plan

As we conclude this chapter on building your essential income plan, it's important to reflect on the peace of mind and security of such planning. A well-structured plan isn't just about numbers and calculations; it's about ensuring a stable, worry-free retirement where your basic needs are met without fail.

Having a clear and reliable plan for your essential expenses means you can face retirement confidently. This confidence comes from knowing that your fundamental needs—housing, food, healthcare, and utilities—will be covered regardless of what happens in the market or the broader economy. It allows you to enjoy the pleasures of retirement, from leisure activities to time with family and friends, without financial stress clouding these golden years.

To maintain this security, it's crucial not only to set up an essential income plan but also to take proactive steps to ensure its effectiveness over time:

- **Stay Informed:** Keep abreast of changes in Social Security, tax laws, and other factors that might affect your retirement income.

- **Flexible Adjustments:** Be prepared to adjust your spending or savings strategies in response to changes in your personal circumstances or the economic environment.

- **Regular Reviews:** Schedule annual financial plan reviews to assess whether your income sources are keeping pace with your expenses. This is especially important for adapting to changes in health needs or living arrangements.

Continual Review and Adjustment

Life is not static, and neither should your retirement plan be. As you progress through different phases of retirement, your needs and external economic conditions will inevitably change. Regularly revisiting and adjusting your essential income plan ensures it remains aligned with your current situation and future goals.

- **Economic Changes:** Economic inflation or deflation can significantly impact your cost of living. Adjust your plan accordingly to ensure your income continues to meet your needs.

- **Health and Mobility Changes:** Health care becomes more critical and potentially costly as you age. Ensure your plan can adapt to increasing medical costs or long-term care needs.

- **Family Dynamics:** Changes in your family structure, such as losing a spouse or new dependents, may require adjustments in your income planning.

The journey to a secure retirement is continuous and often requires adjustments and recalibrations. By establishing a solid foundation with your essential income plan and committing to regular reviews and adjustments, you set the stage for a financially secure retirement rich in opportunities to pursue your passions and interests without monetary worries.

Take these insights and build an essential income plan reflecting your retirement aspirations. With proper planning and proactive management, you can look forward to a future where financial stability is a constant, allowing you to enjoy every moment of your retirement to the fullest.

Make a Difference with Your Review

Share the Gift of Guidance

"Just as sharing a meal can fill another's belly, sharing your thoughts can enrich another's future."

Have you ever wondered how a few minutes of your time could help someone you've never met? Well, here's your chance to find out!

Who needs your help? They're folks just starting their retirement planning journey, unsure of the path, and looking for guidance like you once were.

My mission is simple: to make retirement planning understandable and accessible for everyone. To reach that goal, we need to connect with people everywhere, and we need your help to do it.

Here's where you come in: Many people choose books based on reviews. So, I'm asking you, on behalf of someone out there who needs this knowledge:

Please take a moment to leave a review for "The Retirement Income Equation."

Your review costs nothing and takes less than a minute, but it could change someone's life by helping them secure their financial future. Your words have the power to influence and guide others.

Here's how to leave your review:

Scan the Q.R. code below or visit this link:

https://www.amazon.com/review/review-your-purchases/?asin=B0DCLRV2ST

Imagine the impact your words could have. Your review could help:

- One more retiree enjoys a worry-free retirement.

- One more family feels secure about their financial future.

- One more person sleeps better, knowing they're prepared for what's ahead.

Feel good and help make a difference today. Just a few taps and you're done!

Thank you from the bottom of my heart for your support and time.

Jeff Kikel

Your Stress-Free Retirement Guide

P.S. Remember that sharing valuable insights makes you a hero in someone's story. If this book can help someone you know, why not share it with them, too? Together, we can bring hope and security to many.

Part II: Enhancing Your Lifestyle With Flexibility

Chapter 12

Having Fun With Discretionary Income

"Retirement planning is a dynamic process—keep reviewing, adjusting, and optimizing your strategy."

Let's discuss the fun part of your retirement funds—discretionary income. This is your play money, the cash you get to spend after all the bills are paid and the essentials are covered. It's what you've worked for all these years: the freedom to enjoy life without punching a clock.

What Exactly Is Discretionary Income?

Imagine this: all your needs are met—your house, utilities, groceries, and insurance. What you have left is your discretionary income. It's the money you can spend on the fun stuff—whether traveling to places you've always dreamed of, indulging in hobbies you've never had time for, or simply enjoying a nice dinner whenever the mood strikes. This money lets you live life on your terms in retirement.

Why does this matter? Because retirement should be enjoyable! You've spent your life saving for this phase, and while covering the necessities is critical, the extras make life delightful and full of zest. Here's why discretionary income can make such a big difference:

- **Joy and Satisfaction:** This is your time to savor life's pleasures without guilt. Whether it's a cruise, a golf membership, or tickets to the opera, how you spend your discretionary income can bring tremendous joy and fulfillment.

- **Growth and Exploration:** Ever wanted to paint, learn a new language, or write a book? Now you can. Discretionary funds support your personal growth and let you explore new passions.

- **Keeping Connected:** Staying active socially is easier when you're not worried about every penny. Whether it's a charity event, a community class, or a regular get-together with friends, having the funds to participate keeps you connected and engaged.

Retirement is your time to shine, and discretionary income is the polish. As we move through this chapter, I'll share some strategies to help ensure that you have enough to cover the must-haves and enjoy those nice-to-haves that make life sparkle. We'll talk about finding the right balance so that your golden years are truly golden without sacrificing the security you need.

Planning For Fun Without Compromising Security

Let's discuss how you can have your cake and eat it, too, without compromising your roof over your head or your ability to keep the lights on.

Budgeting for Discretionary Expenses

Setting up a retirement budget isn't just about figuring out how to pay the bills; it's about carving out space for fun. Here's how you can plan to fund your adventures and hobbies without tipping the financial scales:

- **Know What You Love:** List the activities and hobbies you love or want to try. Whether you're passionate about traveling, photography, or fine dining, knowing what you're passionate about helps you prioritize your spending.

- **Set Your Fun Fund:** Allocate a specific portion of your budget for discretionary spending. This is your 'fun fund' – think of it as a dedicated pot for everything that brings you joy.

- **Be Realistic:** It's easy to underestimate how much leisure activities cost. Do a little research to get a sense of what things cost. How much are tickets to the theater? What about a round of golf or a painting class? Getting a realistic picture will help you set a practical, fun fund without overstretching.

- **Flexibility Is Key:** Some months, you might spend more on fun, others less. Keep your budget flexible enough to roll over unused funds from one month to the next. For example, you might save on dining out one month but splurge on a weekend getaway the next.

This approach isn't just about ensuring you have money to spend; it's about ensuring that spending enriches your life without endangering your financial health. Remember, the goal is to enhance your retirement years rather than to exhaust your resources. By budgeting wisely and prioritizing what makes you happy, you can savor your retirement to the fullest.

Next, we'll discuss how you can maximize these fun funds—getting the most bang for your buck, so to speak.

Sources Of Discretionary Income

Utilizing Savings and Investments

Consider retirement the time to finally make your savings and investments serve you, sprinkling extra joy into your life. It's about striking that perfect balance—enjoying the present while watching the future.

Creating a regular income stream from your investments doesn't have to be complicated. You could set up a system where you withdraw a fixed percentage annually, so you know exactly how much you have to spend each year. Another neat trick is the bucket strategy. Imagine dividing your investments into three pots or 'buckets' based on when you'll need to dip into them. The first bucket is for the near future, filled with safer, easy-to-access investments. The second is for the medium term, which is a bit riskier. And the third is your long-term play, aimed at growth.

Pulling money from the correct accounts at the right time can save you a tax bundle. Usually, you'd start with your taxable accounts to keep your tax-deferred accounts growing strong.

Part-Time Work and Passive Income

Retirement is also a fantastic time to earn a bit on the side, especially if it's something you enjoy. It's not just about the money—it's about staying active, engaged, and mentally sharp.

- **Part-Time Work:** You've got a lifetime of skills and experience—why not put that to good use? Consulting in your old field, freelancing, or even picking up seasonal jobs can bring in some extra cash while keeping your days interesting. Plus, it's a great way to meet new people and stay connected to your community.

- **Passive Income Streams:** For a more hands-off approach, consider rental properties or investing in dividend stocks or real estate investment trusts (REITs). These can deliver a steady paycheck without you having to do the daily grind.

Making It Work

The key here is balance. You want these income sources to add to your life, not become a burden. If you're dipping into investments, ensure you're not constantly stressing over the stock market's ups and downs. Choose part-time work that feels more like fun than a job. Remember, this is your time—your retirement should be about enjoying life with some extra security tucked away. Keep things flexible, be ready to adjust your plans as life unfolds, and most importantly, make sure you're having fun doing it!

Making Discretionary Spending More Rewarding

Let's discuss making every dollar of your discretionary income stretch further. It's not just about having money to spend; it's about paying it smartly so you get more bang for your buck.

Stretching Your Dollars

Who doesn't love a good deal? As a senior, you're eligible for various discounts—movies, meals, and travel. Make sure you always ask about senior discounts wherever you go. Traveling during off-peak times saves money and lets you avoid the crowds, making your trips more enjoyable. And don't forget about those loyalty programs. Whether it's airlines, hotels, or even your local coffee shop, these programs can offer fantastic savings and perks.

Prioritizing Experiences

When spending your discretionary income, consider investing in experiences rather than just things. The thrill of a new gadget or piece of clothing fades quickly, but the memories of a great experience can bring joy for years.

Planning for Big-Ticket Experiences

Maybe you've always dreamed of a safari in Africa or a cruise around the Mediterranean. You may want to celebrate a significant anniversary with a huge family gathering. Planning and saving for these types of experiences can be incredibly rewarding. Start by setting goals and then budgeting specifically for these adventures. It's about making those dreams a reality—one smart saving step at a time.

Here's a little tip: sometimes, planning the experience is almost as enjoyable as the event itself. So take your time, savor the planning phase, and get every detail just how you want it. This can enhance your anticipation and, ultimately, your enjoyment of the experience.

Wrapping It Up

With these strategies, your discretionary spending won't just drain your resources; it'll be an investment in your happiness. Smart spending can extend your discretionary income further, and prioritizing experiences over possessions can enhance your overall satisfaction with life in retirement. So go ahead, make those plans, seek out those discounts, and enjoy every moment—after all, you've earned it!

Ensuring Sustainable Discretionary Income

Ensuring that your discretionary income lasts throughout your retirement isn't just a one-time setup; it's an ongoing process that requires attention and adjustment. As years go by, your life circumstances, the economy, and your interests will evolve, as will your financial plans.

Why Regular Reviews Are Crucial:

- **Inflation:** The cost of living will generally rise over time, which means what you can buy with your money today might not stretch as far tomorrow. Regularly adjusting your budget for inflation is critical to maintain your lifestyle.

- **Changing Interests and Lifestyle:** Today's activities may differ from your preference in ten years. You may develop new hobbies that require different spending strategies. When we plan at Freedom Day Wealth with our clients, we typically plan in five-year segments. We find that our clients can predict their fun for that time period, but it gets a little fuzzier as you go farther out.

- **Health Changes:** As you age, your health status may change, potentially increasing medical costs or changing your ability to participate in certain activities, which could affect how you allocate your discretionary funds.

How to Keep Your Discretionary Income Sustainable:

1. **Annual Budget Review:** Set a date each year to go through your discretionary budget. This is the time to adjust for inflation, review your spending habits, and realign your budget with your current interests and lifestyle.

2. **Flexibility in Planning:** Keep your financial plans flexible. Have categories in your budget that can easily be adjusted as your interests shift or as different needs arise.

3. **Consult with Financial Advisors:** As part of your annual review, consider consulting with a financial advisor to get expert insights into economic trends and personal financial health.

Emergency Fund for Unexpected Opportunities

Life is full of surprises; sometimes, those surprises come with a price tag. Whether it's a last-minute travel opportunity, a surprise visit from old friends, or a chance to attend a special event, having a financial cushion can allow you to seize these moments joyfully without the stress of stretching your budget.

Setting Up an Opportunity Fund:

- **Allocate a Portion of Your Income:** Consider setting aside a small part of your monthly discretionary income into a dedicated' opportunity fund'. This isn't your emergency fund for medical expenses or home repairs—it's specifically for unexpected joys.

- **Keep It Accessible:** Make sure this fund is easily accessible. Unlike long-term investments, you'll want to be able to use these funds at short notice without incurring penalties.

- **Regular Contributions:** Treat this fund like any other budget line item. Contributing regularly ensures it grows over time, giving you more freedom to take advantage of opportunities.

Sustainable discretionary income is vital to a fulfilling and stress-free retirement. By planning long-term, regularly reviewing your financial situation, and setting aside money for unexpected opportunities, you can ensure that you have enough money to enjoy day-to-day activities and the flexibility to embrace the spontaneous moments that make life exciting. Retirement should be enjoyed thoroughly, and a well-managed discretionary budget is essential.

Chapter Exercises

Exercise: Lifestyle Prioritization

This exercise is about aligning your spending with your happiness. It will help you pinpoint what truly brings you joy and how best to allocate your discretionary budget to these activities.

What You'll Need:

- A list of activities you enjoy or want to try.

- An estimate of the costs associated with these activities.

- A ranking system (1-10) to gauge your anticipated or experienced enjoyment.

Steps for Lifestyle Prioritization:

1. **List and Cost Your Activities:** Write down all the activities you enjoy or want to try. Next to each, list the approximate cost of engaging in these activities over a month or a year.

2. **Rank Your Enjoyment:** Consider how much joy, satisfaction, or fulfillment each activity brings you. Rate each activity on a scale from 1 to 10, with 10 being the most fulfilling.

3. **Assess Cost vs. Value:** Compare the cost of each activity with the joy it brings. Are there high-cost activities with low enjoyment scores? Or low-cost activities that bring a lot of happiness?

4. **Prioritize Spending:** Based on your assessment, decide which activities deserve more of your budget. Consider cutting back on less fulfilling expenses to save money for those who bring greater joy.

These tools are designed to turn the abstract concept of budgeting into a practical, enjoyable activity that directly contributes to your happiness in retirement. By planning your discretionary spending and aligning it with what brings you the most joy, you ensure that every dollar spent enhances your life. Remember, retirement is the time to live your best life, and managing your finances wisely is a crucial part of that journey.

Conclusion: Embracing The Freedom Of Discretionary Income

As we wrap up this chapter on the joys and strategies of managing discretionary income in retirement, it's clear that this aspect of your financial planning is about much more than just numbers—it's about creating and embracing a life filled with enjoyment, growth, and unexpected pleasures.

Discretionary income is your key to unlocking a vibrant and fulfilling retirement. It allows you to explore new hobbies, travel, engage in social activities, and indulge in passions that perhaps took a back seat during your working years. But the freedom it offers is best enjoyed when it's managed with foresight and prudence.

Key Takeaways from the Chapter

- **Balanced Spending:** We've discussed how balancing fun spending with financial prudence is crucial. It's about ensuring that your enjoyment today doesn't compromise your security tomorrow.

- **Innovative Strategies:** Smart strategies help maximize the value of discretionary funds, from utilizing discounts and off-peak travel benefits to engaging in part-time work or managing investments.

- **Long-term Sustainability:** Regularly reviewing and adjusting your plans to cope with inflation, changing interests, and health is essential to maintain the sustainability of your discretionary income.

- **Opportunity Fund:** Setting aside some of your funds for spontaneous joys ensures that unexpected opportunities can be embraced without financial stress.

Moving Forward

Remember these strategies as you move forward into the deeper waters of retirement. Adapting and being flexible with your spending plans will serve you well. Retirement is not just a phase of life; it's a dynamic continuation of your journey, filled with potential for personal development and joy.

Consider this chapter a foundation for understanding how to effectively manage the discretionary portion of your retirement income. It's a guide to help you make informed decisions that enhance the quality of your life. Whether traveling to unseen parts of the world, picking up new or long-lost hobbies, or simply enjoying the local life and community events, how you spend your discretionary income can transform your retirement years.

Encourage yourself to revisit these concepts regularly, adjust as necessary, and always watch for opportunities to make your retirement even more rewarding. With the right plans, your golden years can be truly golden.

Chapter 13

Creating Your Discretionary Income Plan

"Your retirement is a marathon, not a sprint. Pace yourself, plan well, and enjoy the journey."

Welcome to the nuts and bolts of managing your fun money—discretionary income. Before we dive into the specifics of bond ladders and sinking funds, let's revisit what we mean by discretionary income. This is the portion of your finances set aside for the joys of life in retirement: travel, hobbies, dining out, and more. It's about spending on the pleasures that make life rich and fulfilling beyond the basic necessities.

While it's exciting to think about the freedom this money offers, managing it with a structured plan is equally essential. This ensures your fun fund is sustainable and sufficient to support your desired lifestyle throughout retirement.

The Role of Structured Planning

Having a structured approach to managing your discretionary income is crucial. It ensures you have a steady stream of funds available for your enjoyment without compromising your essential financial needs. In my planning with clients, I typically use a 5-year bond ladder to plan for discretionary income. A bond ladder buys equal amounts of bonds with maturities starting from 1 - 5 years, each maturing annually. This chapter will discuss this and the concept of a sinking fund.

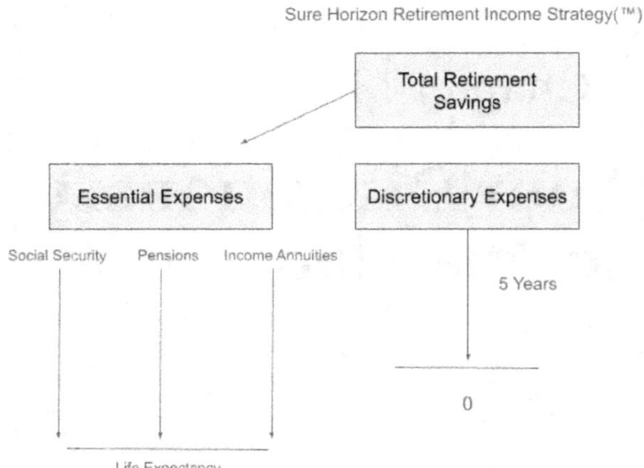

For over 30 years, I've helped clients set up Discretionary Income Strategies using bond ladders because they are straightforward, cost-effective, and easy to understand—even for those who aren't financial wizards. A bond ladder allows you to allocate savings for specific future expenses and manage these funds in a way that reduces risk and increases predictability.

Expanding the Toolkit

While we focus on bond ladders, remember that they are just one of many tools available to manage your discretionary funds. As discussed in the previous chapter, you might also consider mutual funds, real estate investments, or even maintaining a part-time job. Each can supplement your income, providing more flexibility and opportunities to enjoy retirement.

As we move forward, we'll define a bond ladder and a sinking fund and explain how you can effectively use them to enhance your discretionary income strategy. This approach will make managing your fun money more accessible and more rewarding.

5 Year Sinking Fund Strategy

A sinking fund is a strategic financial tool for accumulating money and planning its use in a structured way. Think of it as your budgeting buddy for significant or recurring expenses. In retirement, we use a sinking fund primarily for managing discretionary spending—those non-essential but life-enriching expenses that make retirement enjoyable.

The beauty of a sinking fund lies in its simplicity and effectiveness. It allows you to set aside a specific amount of money regularly to fund future expenditures without unexpectedly dipping into your primary savings. This method benefits retirees who want to plan their leisure activities without financial stress.

Using a Bond Ladder in a Sinking Fund

One of the most efficient ways to structure a sinking fund for discretionary income is through a bond ladder. A bond ladder is a portfolio of fixed-income securities, with each bond having a different maturity date. The staggered maturities provide a reliable, predictable income stream over a set period—ideal for our purpose, typically around five years.

How It Works:

- **Staggered Maturities:** You purchase bonds that mature in one, two, three, four, and five years. This setup ensures that one of your bonds will mature each year, releasing a certain amount of capital you can use for your discretionary spending.

- **Reliable Income:** As each bond matures annually, you receive its face value along with the last interest payment it accrues. This provides a predictable and steady income stream to fund your lifestyle without impacting the rest of your investment portfolio. When we build bond ladders for clients, we typically use a combination of U.S. Treasuries and Investment-Grade Corporate Bonds.

- **Reducing Reinvestment Risk:** Having bonds with staggered maturities minimizes the risk of reinvesting a large sum of money when interest rates may be unfavorable. Each year, only a portion of your investment needs to be reinvested.

Benefits of This Approach:

- **Smoothing Income Fluctuations:** The regular maturation of bonds in a ladder creates a smoother income stream, making it easier to manage cash flow for leisure activities.

- **Flexibility:** The bond ladder strategy provides flexibility as you can choose the types and durations of bonds based on your income needs and risk tolerance.

- **Simplicity:** Once set up, a bond ladder requires minimal maintenance, allowing you to enjoy your retirement without worrying about managing this part of your portfolio too frequently.

By integrating a bond ladder into your sinking fund strategy, you can enjoy your retirement years with the assurance that your discretionary spending is well-funded and predictable. This method secures your financial needs for fun and leisure. It does so in a way that's easy to understand and implement, even for those who aren't financial experts.

Setting Up a Bond Ladder

Let's talk about setting up your bond ladder, like crafting a tailor-made playlist for your retirement income. You want this playlist to have just the right mix of tunes (or bonds, in this case) that play at just the correct times, giving you a steady stream of income to fund all those fun activities you've planned.

Choosing Your Bonds

Picking bonds for your ladder isn't just grabbing anything off the shelf. You've got options, and your choices should match your risk tolerance and income needs:

- **Treasury Bonds:** Consider these as the old classics—reliable and steady. They don't pay much but are about as safe as possible. However, the treasury market is the most significant and liquid global market. There is a welcome and open market if you need to liquidate.

- **Corporate Bonds:** These are a bit like jazz—more variation, potentially more rewarding, but definitely riskier. The financial health of the company you're lending to can affect your returns. Most major companies are pretty liquid if you need to sell; however, that is not true for all Corporate Bonds.

- **Municipal Bonds:** If tax-free income sounds good to you (and probably does), these bonds are worth looking at. They fund things like schools and highways and are relatively safe, although not as rock-solid as Treasuries.

It would help if you also considered how long each bond will run. Matching the bond's duration with your cash flow needs is critical. It only makes sense to lock away your money in a 30-year bond if you'll need it in five years.

Setting the Timing

Timing your bond maturities is like setting up reminders for important dates—they ensure you've always got cash on hand when needed. Suppose you set them up to mature annually. In that case, you'll know you have a consistent income once a year, which, in our strategy, gives you a lump sum of money at the beginning of each year that you will use to fund your "fun expenses."

Figuring Out What You'll Make

While the income we earn from the bond ladder is irrelevant to the overall strategy (we are mainly looking at the maturing principal), let's break down how much you can expect to earn from your bond ladder. You'll want to look at:

- **Yield:** This is what your bond pays you in interest. Higher yields often come with higher risks, so balance is critical.

- **Face Value:** The amount you'll get back when the bond matures. It's the 'principal' part of your investment.

- **Cash Flow Timing:** Knowing exactly when each bond will pay out lets you plan your spending better. For example, if a bond pays out in June, you might plan a summer vacation using that cash.

Here's a simple way to think: If you invest $20,000 in a bond with a 3% yield, you'll pay about $600 a year just in interest. When the bond matures, you get your $20,000 back, which you can reinvest, spend, or save.

Setting up a bond ladder for your Discretionary Income is like setting up a financial safety net that ensures you keep getting paid regularly, just like when you were working. It's about making sure you have enough money coming in regularly to enjoy your retirement without worrying about economic and financial market changes. Remember, the key to a successful bond ladder is keeping it aligned with your life—your needs, goals, and dreams.

Rebuilding the Ladder:

In our strategy, rather than continuously reinvesting each bond as it matures, we let the ladder run its course over five years. Once the last bond pays out, it's time for a reboot. This is when you take a portion of the capital from the growth segment of your Retirement Income Plan to replenish the bond ladder.

When you rebuild the ladder every five years, it's an excellent opportunity to adjust your budget for discretionary spending. This is when you can account for any changes in your living costs due to inflation or shifts in your lifestyle. You may spend more on hobbies or travel or scale back a bit.

Flexibility in Reinvestment:

The market conditions when your bonds mature will guide what you do next. If bond rates are favorable, you might rebuild the ladder just as it was or even expand it. Consider other income-generating assets if rates are down or there are better opportunities elsewhere. This could mean supplementing your bond ladder with dividend stocks, mutual funds, or even real estate, depending on what fits best with your overall financial plan.

Integrating Your Plan With An Overall Retirement Strategy

Holistic Financial Planning

When piecing together a retirement plan, think of it as crafting a mosaic—each part needs to fit perfectly with the others to create a cohesive picture. Your discretionary income plan, including your bond ladder, isn't an island; it's deeply interconnected with every other financial decision you make.

Fitting the Pieces Together:

The first piece of the puzzle is your essential income—your guaranteed income covering non-negotiables like housing, food, and healthcare. It's your financial bedrock.

Then comes your discretionary income plan. This is where your bond ladder shines, managing the money you use for life's fun and fulfilling parts. It needs to sync with your essential income, ensuring that your basics are covered so everything else is discretionary.

Think of it this way, if your essential income is about survival, your discretionary income is about enjoyment. One keeps you secure, and the other makes that security worthwhile.

Flexibility in Planning

No matter how well you plan, life has a way of throwing curveballs. Your retirement plan needs to be as flexible as a gymnast, bending without breaking, no matter what comes your way.

Why Flexibility Matters:

- **Lifestyle Changes:** What you enjoy or need can change as years pass by. You could take up golf or travel less and spend more time with your grandchildren. Your discretionary spending needs to be able to pivot towards what matters most to you at any given time.

- **Unexpected Expenses:** Sometimes, things don't go as planned—a significant home repair might crop up, or a medical issue may arise. If your plan is rigid, these expenses can throw your budget off balance. Flexibility allows you to handle these surprises without toppling your financial security.

- **Opportunities:** Occasionally, opportunities come up that you didn't anticipate, like a dream trip or a chance to invest in a passion project. If your plan has some give, you can seize these without guilt or worry.

Integrating your discretionary income plan into your overall retirement strategy is about more than just finances; it's about ensuring that your retirement is as prosperous in enjoyment as it is in security. It's about having the freedom to adapt, the stability to handle life's ups and downs, and the foresight to see your retirement as a dynamic, evolving phase of life. With a well-integrated plan, you're not just surviving your retirement years—you're thriving.

Chapter Exercises

Exercise: Evaluate Your Discretionary Spending Needs

It's crucial to match your income strategy with your actual spending needs. This exercise will help you evaluate your anticipated discretionary spending and match it to the income generated from your bond ladder.

Steps for Evaluating Discretionary Spending Needs:

1. **List Discretionary Spending Categories:** List all potential discretionary spending categories such as travel, hobbies, dining out, and entertainment.

2. **Estimate Annual Spending:** For each category, estimate how much you expect

to spend annually. Be realistic and consider any changes you anticipate in your lifestyle.

3. **Match with Bond Income:** Using the income calculations from your Bond Ladder Planner, align your anticipated spending with the income from each bond's maturity. This will help you see if your budget has gaps or surpluses.

4. **Adjust as Needed:** If your income from the bond ladder needs to fully cover your discretionary spending needs, consider adjusting your bond investments or reevaluating your spending priorities.

The Bond Ladder Planner and the Discretionary Spending Needs exercise are designed to give you greater control and confidence in managing your retirement finances. By aligning your income sources with your spending desires, these tools ensure that your retirement is financially stable and richly rewarding.

> If you have not already done so, please go to the companion website for this book, www.SureHorizonRetirement.com/Toolkit, and download our FREE Toolkit to follow along with the exercises.

Wrapping It Up: The Bond Ladder Strategy

As we conclude this chapter on structuring a bond ladder to manage your discretionary income in retirement, let's recap the essential points and set the stage for expanding your financial toolkit in the next chapter.

Throughout this discussion, we've explored the practical aspects of using a bond ladder as a sinking fund. This method helps provide predictable and steady income to fund your retirement life's enjoyable, non-essential parts. From selecting the suitable types of bonds to timing their maturities to match your spending needs, we've covered how to set up a system that supports your current lifestyle and adapts to changing economic conditions and personal preferences.

Key Takeaways:

- **Structured Planning:** The bond ladder strategy emphasizes the importance of having a structured approach to manage discretionary income effectively, ensuring it remains sustainable and aligned with your overall retirement plan.

- **Flexibility and Adjustment:** We've highlighted the need for flexibility in planning. You should be able to adjust your bond ladder in response to changes in interest rates, financial goals, or personal circumstances.

- **Holistic Financial Planning:** The bond ladder is part of a broader financial strategy that includes other income sources and investment techniques, ensuring a well-rounded approach to funding your retirement.

Looking Ahead: Beyond the Bond Ladder

The next chapter, "Beyond the Bond Ladder: Other Sources of Discretionary Income," explores additional methods to enhance your discretionary spending capabilities. While bond ladders offer a great start, diversifying your sources of income can provide further stability and opportunities to enjoy your retirement to the fullest.

What to Expect:

- **Exploring Alternatives:** We'll explore other investment vehicles and strategies to complement or enhance the bond ladder approach. This includes mutual funds, real estate investments, and dividend stocks.

- **Adapting to New Opportunities:** The financial landscape is constantly evolving, and so should your retirement planning. We'll discuss how to stay adaptable and take advantage of emerging opportunities that can boost your discretionary income.

- **Integrating New Strategies:** Learn how to incorporate these new income sources into your existing financial plan without disrupting your current setup.

As we move forward, remember that managing your retirement finances is more than just covering needs—it's about creating opportunities to live a rich and fulfilling life in your golden years. Join us in the next chapter as we explore innovative and effective ways to enhance your financial freedom in retirement.

Chapter 14
Beyond The Bond Ladder

"Your retirement income must work as hard as you did to earn it. Ensure every dollar has a purpose."

Welcome to the realm of broadening your financial horizons! While 'bond ladders ', a strategy where you invest in a series of bonds with different maturity dates, are a fantastic tool for generating predictable, steady income during retirement, they are just one part of a larger picture. It's like having a favorite fishing spot; it's reliable, but exploring different waters can sometimes yield even better catches. This chapter is about expanding your income options to enhance both financial stability and the enjoyment of your retirement years.

Expanding Income Options

Imagine your retirement income as a portfolio of photographs. Each picture represents a different source of income, and together, they create a diverse and colorful album. While bond ladders provide:

- A solid, reliable base image.

- Diversifying your income sources adds richness and depth.

- Ensuring you have a well-rounded financial picture.

Why settle for just one approach when you can benefit from multiple? By diversifying your income streams, you not only bolster your financial stability but also open up new opportunities to enjoy your retirement to its fullest. This diversification provides a safety net, ensuring that you're still secure even if one income source falters.

Purpose of Diverse Income Streams

Diversifying your income sources isn't just about having more—it's more innovative, flexible options. Here's why it's crucial:

- **Risk Management:** Just as investors diversify their investment portfolios to manage risk, diversifying your income sources helps protect against the economic downturns that might affect one particular income stream.

- **Increased Income Potential:** Different sources of income may have different growth potentials. Having multiple streams can mean more funds are available, giving you the freedom to explore, enjoy, and invest in your retirement dreams.

- **Flexibility:** With various income sources, you can adjust based on performance, economic conditions, and personal needs. If one stream diminishes, others can fill the gap, ensuring your lifestyle isn't dramatically affected.

- **Tax Advantages:** One of the advantages of dividend investing is how dividends are taxed. Taxing authorities want people to take risks and invest in companies, so dividend distributions are taxed at a lower tax rate (maximum of 20% in the U.S.). Rates can be even lower if you are in a lower tax bracket. This tax advantage is similar in other countries around the world.

In this chapter, we'll explore a variety of alternative income sources, from investments in real estate and dividend stocks to part-time entrepreneurship and more. Each offers unique advantages and can be crucial to your Retirement Income Strategy. Adding some or all of these sources will put less stress on your investment portfolio, specifically for Discretionary Expenses, ensuring your retirement is as dynamic and secure as it is enjoyable. Let's dive in and discover how these alternatives can contribute to a more prosperous, diversified retirement plan. The potential for growth and excitement in exploring these options is immense.

Dividend Income

Let's discuss one of the most appealing sources of passive income for retirees—dividends. Imagine owning a part of a company that pays you regularly just for holding onto its shares. That's essentially what dividends are: payments made to shareholders from a corporation's earnings. Whether these come from stocks, mutual funds, or ETFs (Exchange-Traded Funds), dividends can provide a steady stream of income, which is particularly attractive during retirement.

Benefits of Dividend-Paying Securities:

- **Consistent Income:** Dividends provide regular payouts, which can be quarterly, semi-annually, or annually, depending on the company or fund's policy. This regularity can help supplement your retirement income.

- **Income Growth through Reinvestment:** One of the great features of dividend income is the ability to reinvest those dividends to purchase more shares. Over time, this can lead to compounding growth, increasing your investment value and dividend income.

- **Potential for Stability and Appreciation:** Companies that pay dividends are often more stable and established. While dividends provide income, these stocks can also offer capital appreciation over the long term.

Building a Dividend Portfolio

Creating a portfolio of dividend-paying securities isn't just about picking stocks with the highest yields. It's about strategic selection and management to ensure a steady income, risk management, and growth potential. This process puts you in control of your financial future, empowering you to make informed decisions.

Selecting Dividend-Paying Securities:

- **Dividend Yield:** A stock's annual dividend payments divided by its price. Going for high yields is tempting, but they can sometimes be unsustainable. Look for a balance between attractive yield and safety.

- **Dividend Stability and Growth:** Check the company's dividend history. A promising sign is a steady or increasing dividend payout over many years, which suggests financial health and reliability.

- **Sector Diversification:** To mitigate risks associated with any single economic sector, diversify your holdings across different sectors. This way, if one sector experiences a downturn, your entire income stream isn't jeopardized.

Tips for Diversification:

- **Spread Investments:** Don't put all your eggs in one basket. Spread your investments across various industries such as utilities, consumer goods, and technology—all of which have different market dynamics.

- **Geographical Diversification:** Consider international dividend-paying stocks or funds. They can provide diversification benefits and potential exposure to faster-growing economies.

Dividends can be a golden source of income for retirees, offering both the joy of regular income and the potential for your investment to grow. By carefully selecting and managing a diversified portfolio of dividend stocks, you can enjoy a more secure and prosperous retirement. Remember, the goal isn't just to collect checks and strategically grow and protect your retirement funds.

So, what can you expect to earn from a dividend portfolio? The S&P 500 average, as of this writing, is 1.33% below its long-term average of 1.8%. I don't know about you, but that doesn't really get me excited because it means that I have to count on my dividend-paying stocks growing 8% per year to get to the long-term average total return of close to 10%.

In the portfolios we run for clients at my firm, we have a strategy called the 'Income Machine '. This strategy focuses mainly on Senior Secured Credit, Collateralized Loan Obligations (CLOs), and Business Development Corporations (BDCs). With this strategy, we flip the dividend world backward and look for things with relatively little or no capital growth but pay most of their profits out in dividends. This allows us to predict income coming in for our clients and reduce market risk. As a result, we can get average yields up in the 10-11% range. Using this type of strategy is not 'Fire and Forget.' It requires diligence and research to ensure that the investments continue generating the expected income.

I learned this style of investing from my mentor, Steven Bavaria, through his columns on www.seekingalpha.com and through his excellent book *The Income Factory* (Bavaria, Steven. *The Income Factory: An Investor's Guide to Consistent Lifetime Returns*. Mc-Graw-Hill Education, 2020.) We took Steven's basic strategy and adapted it to our style of investing at our firm, and it has done wonders for client portfolios. This book is a wonderful start if you want to add a dividend strategy to your discretionary income pools.

Income From Real Estate

If you're looking for a way to generate significant discretionary income during retirement, diving into real estate might be your ticket. Whether it's residential or commercial properties, real estate investments can provide a robust stream of rental income that enhances your lifestyle and diversifies your income sources beyond the typical stock and bond investments.

Why Consider Real Estate:

- **Steady Cash Flow:** Rental properties can provide a regular, predictable income, much like receiving a paycheck, except this one comes from your tenants.

- **Appreciation Potential:** Over time, real estate typically increases in value. This means you could sell the property for more than you paid and collect rent along the way.

- **Tax Advantages:** Real estate investing offers various tax benefits, such as deductions for mortgage interest, property taxes, maintenance costs, and depreciation.

Managing Rental Properties

While the benefits of owning rental properties are compelling, effectively managing them is critical to ensuring they turn out to be a blessing, not a burden. Here's how to stay on top of things and make the most of your real estate investments.

Choosing the Right Properties:

- **Location, Location, Location:** The adage holds true. The location of your property significantly affects both the rental income you can charge and the property's appreciation potential. Look for areas with growing job markets, good schools, and amenities.

- **Property Type and Condition:** Consider what type of property you want to invest in—single-family homes, apartments, or commercial properties. Each comes with different management needs and investment potentials. Also, assess the condition of the property to avoid costly repairs that can eat into your profits.

Handling Tenants:

- **Finding Good Tenants:** Good tenants can make your life as a landlord much more accessible. Conduct thorough background and credit checks to ensure your tenants are reliable and likely to pay rent on time.

- **Tenant Relationships:** Keeping a good relationship with your tenants can lead to more extended stays and fewer vacancies. Be responsive to their needs and address maintenance issues promptly.

Dealing with Maintenance and Emergencies:

- **Regular Maintenance:** Keeping your property well-maintained helps retain its value and keeps tenants happy. Set up a regular maintenance schedule for landscaping, checking appliances, and ensuring safety measures are in place.

- **Emergency Fund:** Always have a fund set aside for emergency repairs. Plumbing issues or heating failures can happen unexpectedly and need immediate attention to keep the property habitable.

Investing in rental properties can be rewarding because it generates discretionary income during retirement. Still, it requires active management and a strategic approach. My personal strategy for any rental properties we own is to hire a professional management company to run them for us. We build that into our investment structure to be profitable but make our investment in the property genuinely passive.

By understanding the responsibilities and setting up the proper management practices, you can enjoy the benefits of real estate investment while minimizing the potential stresses and risks. Whether you dive deep into real estate or dip your toes in, remember that knowledge and preparation are crucial to success, like any investment.

Part-Time Work

Who says retirement means you have to stop working? For many, retirement is the perfect time to shift gears from full-time to part-time, blending work with more freedom. Part-time work or consulting in retirement isn't just about supplementing your income—it can be a vital component of a fulfilling, engaging lifestyle.

My dad is an excellent example of this. After spending the first 7-10 years after retirement traveling around the world with my mom, checking things off their bucket list, they reached a point where they didn't enjoy long trips anymore. At age 75, he decided to go back to work at a local big box hardware store. He is a highly trained quality control engineer with over 45 years of experience helping large corporations design quality improvement programs. Today, he works in the hardware aisle of the store and has a ball. Why? Because he has been a committed do-it-yourselfer his entire life and knows how to fix stuff. He works 20-25 hours a week and uses the money he makes for fun. If you are ever at the Lowes in Arlington, Texas, and need some help on a project, ask for Ken and tell him I sent you, and he will get you taken care of. He is a talker, so you will be there for a while.

Imagine continuing to do something YOU love but on your terms and schedule. That's what part-time work in retirement can offer. It keeps you sharp, connects you with others, and can give you a great sense of purpose. Whether you're contributing to a project, sharing your lifetime of knowledge as a consultant, or just staying in the game, the benefits extend well beyond the paycheck.

Finding Suitable Work

How do you find the proper part-time work that feels more like a choice than a chore? Here's what you need to consider:

- **Work Should Align with Your Interests:** Think about what you love doing.

Tax preparation or bookkeeping could be your thing if you've always had a knack for numbers. Loved your years in education? Tutoring could be rewarding. Finding something that feels like something other than work because you enjoy it.

- **Be Mindful of the Physical Demands:** Let's be honest—what you could handle at 30 might not be so comfortable at 60 or 70. Look for jobs that fit your current lifestyle and physical capabilities. The goal is to add to your life, not create stress or strain.

- **Embrace the World of Remote Work:** The internet has revolutionized work possibilities. Many jobs can now be done anywhere, even from the comfort of your home. This can be particularly appealing if commuting doesn't excite you anymore.

- **Flexibility Is Your Friend:** One of the biggest perks of part-time work in retirement should be flexibility. You may want to work mornings and have your afternoons free, or you may prefer working just a few days a week. Look for opportunities that let you enjoy work and leisure time to the fullest.

Part-time work during retirement is really about balancing income with engagement. It's about staying active, involved, and mentally stimulated. It's not just about making money; it's about making these years as enriching and fulfilling as possible. Choose roles that resonate with your interests and respect your pace of life. You can enhance your financial independence with the right job while keeping life vibrant and exciting.

Starting A Home-Based Business

Retirement could be the launch pad for your next great adventure—a home-based or online business. With the wealth of experience accumulated over the years, retirees are uniquely positioned to turn their knowledge and passions into profitable ventures. Starting your own business enhances your income and keeps you intellectually engaged and emotionally invested in your pursuits.

Leveraging Your Expertise

Think about the skills and knowledge you've honed over your career or personal interests that you're passionate about. Whether crafting, consulting, writing, or digital marketing, your expertise can be the foundation for a business that fits your retirement lifestyle. The beauty of a home-based or online business is its scalability—you can start small without the overhead of a physical store or office and expand at your pace.

Building on Proven Strategies

In my other book, *Overcoming The Retirement Trap: An 8-Step Financial Freedom Blueprint for Your Journey to Building Wealth, Creating Financial Independence, and Living a Life Beyond Limits*, I delve into how Pre-retirees and those in retirement can leverage their skills and resources to build cash flow-producing assets. This book can be a valuable resource when planning your business, offering strategies to manage risks, maximize income, and ensure your business survives and thrives.

Practical Steps to Get Started

- **Identify Your Niche:** Your business should reflect something you're passionate about but also something that fills a market need. Do some research to see where your interests and market opportunities align.

- **Develop a Business Plan:** Outline your business goals, target audience, marketing strategy, and financial projections. A solid plan will help guide your decisions and can be crucial for securing funding.

- **Set Up Your Workspace:** One of the perks of a home-based business is working from your own space. Set up a dedicated area that inspires productivity and creativity.

- **Go Digital:** With an online business, your potential market is vast. Ensure you have a user-friendly website and strong social media presence to connect with customers and market your products or services.

- **Stay Compliant:** Understand the legal requirements for running a business from home, including licenses, permits, and tax obligations.

Starting a home-based or online business in retirement isn't just about money; it's about creating something valuable that enhances your life. It's about continuing to grow, learn, and contribute. Your retirement can be some of your most productive and fulfilling years if you step into the role of an entrepreneur with a clear plan and a passion for what you do. With the right approach, you can turn your retirement into an exciting new chapter of creativity and independence.

Chapter Exercises

Understanding your potential for generating alternative income is crucial. This exercise is designed to help you examine your assets, skills, and interests to identify viable income opportunities.

Steps for Evaluating Potential for Alternative Income:

- **Assess Your Assets:** What assets do you have that could generate income? Do you own stocks that pay dividends? Can you rent out a property or a portion of your home?

- **Skillset and Interests:** What skills do you possess that could be monetized? Are you an excellent writer, a seasoned marketer, or a gifted carpenter? Match your skills and interests with potential part-time jobs or freelance opportunities.

- **Lifestyle Compatibility:** Consider how each potential income stream fits your desired lifestyle. How much time will you dedicate to a new business or side job? Are you interested in the day-to-day management of a rental property, or would you prefer something less hands-on?

Reflection Questions:

1. Which income sources are most aligned with my current financial needs and future goals?

2. What are the potential barriers to entering each type of income stream, and how might I overcome them?

How do these income opportunities fit with my overall retirement planning?

The purpose of these tools is not just to map out potential income sources but to integrate them into a broader, holistic approach to retirement planning. By carefully evaluating each opportunity, you can build a diversified portfolio of income streams that not only bolsters your financial security but also enriches your life in retirement.

Wrap-Up: Expanding Your Retirement Income Horizons

As we wrap up this chapter on exploring alternative sources of discretionary income, we've ventured beyond traditional savings and investment strategies like bond ladders to uncover a wealth of opportunities that can enrich your retirement experience. Each option has advantages and challenges, from dividend income and rental properties to part-time work and starting your own business. Still, all aim to enhance your financial flexibility and overall quality of life during retirement.

Embracing Diverse Income Streams

Diversifying your income sources is like diversifying an investment portfolio—balancing risk and reward while aligning with your personal goals and lifestyle. By embracing a mix of passive and active income streams, you create a robust financial foundation that can withstand market fluctuations and personal changes throughout your retirement years.

The Path Forward

As you move forward, remember that retirement is as much about financial security as personal fulfillment. The income strategies discussed here are not just mechanisms for generating cash; they are tools to help you live a rich, engaged, and satisfying life. Whether you invest in real estate, delve into the stock market, or start a small business, each step should be taken with your financial and personal well-being in mind.

Next Steps

Consider the insights and strategies from this chapter as starting points. Evaluate your current financial situation, future income needs, and personal interests to determine which options best suit your retirement plan. Use the exercises and worksheets provided to carefully plan and implement your chosen income strategies. Always be open to revisiting and revising your plans as circumstances evolve—flexibility is critical to maintaining stability and satisfaction in retirement.

Looking Ahead

In the next chapter, we'll explore how to effectively manage these diverse income streams, ensuring they work harmoniously to support your retirement goals. We'll provide guidance on balancing risk, optimizing returns, and adjusting strategies over time to reflect your changing needs and opportunities.

Chapter 15

Adjusting For Life's Changes

"Your retirement strategy should be as dynamic as the world around you. Keep it flexible and adaptable."

Welcome to a chapter that embraces one of the most fundamental truths about retirement: it is as dynamic and evolving as any other phase of life. Gone are the days when retirement was viewed as a static, unchanging period. Today, it's recognized as a time of growth, adaptation, and continual evolution, shaped by personal experiences, economic shifts, and changing aspirations. As the theme of this section of the book is flexibility, this chapter will help you adapt and adjust to what life throws at you.

Dynamic Nature of Retirement

Retirement should be seen not as a final destination but as a vibrant journey that continues to evolve. Like any other stage in life, it requires adjustments and shifts in strategy. Your retirement plan is a living document, not something you write once and file away. It must reflect changes in your lifestyle, health status, family dynamics, and financial markets. Maintaining this flexibility empowers you to navigate life's uncertainties confidently.

Why Flexibility Matters:

- **Personal Changes:** Health, interests, and family situations can change significantly over the years. Your retirement plan must be flexible enough to accommodate these changes, ensuring it always serves your best interests.

- **Economic Conditions:** Financial markets and economic conditions can fluctuate dramatically. A flexible retirement plan allows you to adjust your strategies in response to these changes, protecting your financial well-being against market volatility and economic downturns.

Purpose of Periodic Reviews

Regularly reviewing your retirement plan is not just a suggestion. It's a necessity. It ensures your strategies are effective and in line with your current needs, desires, and the world around you. This is especially crucial for your plan's discretionary and growth components, where flexibility is paramount.

Benefits of Periodic Reviews:

- **Stay Relevant:** Regularly updating your plan ensures it matches your current life situation and future aspirations. What made sense at retirement might not be appropriate after a decade or more.

- **Optimize Resources:** Continuous review helps you maximize your financial resources. It allows you to adjust your spending, saving, and investment strategies to ensure your finances are secure and efficiently utilized.

An up-to-date retirement plan that reflects your current circumstances can bring a profound sense of peace. It reassures you that you're prepared for life's uncertainties, allowing you to focus on enjoying your retirement to the fullest. This chapter will explore how to maintain flexibility in your retirement plan, focusing on the discretionary and growth elements. We will also discuss how regular reviews can help you adjust smoothly to life's inevitable changes. This approach not only safeguards your financial security but also enhances your ability to enjoy this rewarding phase of life to the fullest.

Strategies For Periodic Review

Just as you might schedule regular maintenance for a car or a home to keep everything running smoothly, it's crucial to set regular check-ups for your retirement plan. These reviews help ensure your financial strategies are current and fully optimized for your ever-evolving life circumstances.

Frequency of Reviews:

- **Annual Reviews:** Review your retirement plan at least once a year. This annual check-up should coincide with significant yearly financial events, such as the receipt of tax documents, which can provide a clear picture of your financial health over the past year.

- **Semi-Annual or Quarterly Reviews:** During significant economic fluctuations or major personal life changes (like health issues or family dynamics shifting), it might be wise to increase the frequency of your reviews. This ensures that necessary adjustments are made promptly, keeping your plan responsive and resilient.

In my financial practice, we conduct Quarterly reviews with clients. We have an agenda each quarter that focuses on themes. These may include Insurance reviews, beneficiaries, gifting, taxes, investment returns, etc. I would encourage you to at least review your investment quarterly to ensure you are on target and adjusting to the market environment. You will want to compare the performance of your portfolio with a broad-based market benchmark such as the S&P 500 or the Russell 3000. Although quoted on the news every night, the Dow Jones Industrial Index only represents 30 Mega cap stocks, and the Nasdaq 100 is largely dominated by newer high-tech companies.

Checklist for Review

A structured approach is helpful to make these reviews as effective as possible. A comprehensive checklist can guide you through the review process, ensuring every critical element is noticed.

Components of the Review Checklist:

- **Income Sources:** Examine the stability and sustainability of your income streams. Are dividends, rentals, or part-time work proceeds as expected? Are there new opportunities or emerging risks?

- **Expense Levels:** Review your spending patterns. Have your living costs increased due to inflation? Are there new expenses, like healthcare costs, that must be accounted for?

- **Investment Performance:** Assess your investments' performance. Are they yielding expected returns? Is the risk level still appropriate for your stage in retirement?

- **Significant Life Changes:** Reflect on any significant life events since your last review, such as a marriage in the family, the birth of a grandchild, or the loss of a loved one. Consider how these changes affect your financial needs and goals.

- **Estate Planning Updates:** Ensure your estate plans, including wills and trusts, are current. Changes in legislation or family structure can impact these arrangements.

- **Health Status Changes:** Consider how changes in your health may affect your future medical expenses and care needs. Adjust your healthcare budget and insurance coverage accordingly.

By setting regular intervals for reviewing your retirement plan and following a thorough checklist, you can maintain a plan that meets your current needs and anticipates future changes. This proactive approach allows you to adjust flexibly and quickly, ensuring your retirement is enjoyable and stress-free. It's not just about reacting to changes—it's about anticipating them and planning accordingly. Hence, you continue to thrive no matter what life throws your way, feeling prepared and calm.

Responding To Common Life Changes

Health Changes

Health is a pivotal factor in retirement planning, and changes often come unexpectedly and have significant financial implications. Whether it's a new diagnosis, a change in mobility, or the need for long-term care, health shifts can drastically alter your expenses and income potential.

Strategies for Adjusting Financial Plans:

- **Healthcare Budgeting:** If you're facing increased medical costs, it's essential to reassess your healthcare budget. Consider reallocating funds from less critical areas or expanding your healthcare fund to cover these expenses. This may include reallocating some money from the Discretionary pool to create an additional guaranteed income stream in your Essential pool. In that case, the easiest thing to do is shift some money to buy another income annuity. This will ensure that it lasts as long as you do.

- **Long-term Care Insurance:** If you haven't already, explore options for long-term care insurance. This can help cover the costs of assisted living or home care, protecting your savings from substantial medical expenses. We will cover Long-Term Care in much more detail in a bonus chapter at the end of the book.

- **Accessible Investments:** Ensure that your investment plan accommodates your physical capabilities. For instance, if managing real estate becomes too demanding, consider more passive income streams that require less day-to-day involvement.

Family Needs

Family dynamics can shift dramatically during retirement, from financial support for a child or grandchild to the emotional and economic implications of losing a spouse. Each change requires a thoughtful adjustment to your retirement strategy.

Incorporating Family Changes:

- **Emergency Fund:** Strengthen or establish an emergency fund that can handle sudden financial responsibilities, like supporting a family member.

- **Estate Reevaluation:** Losing a spouse or another family member may necessitate changes to your estate plans. Make sure your will, trusts, and beneficiary designations reflect your current family structure. This should be reviewed annually, at the very least. After 30 years of working with clients, I can tell you horror stories about family changes and failing to update beneficiaries, especially in the case of divorce.

- **Flexible Income Planning:** Adjust your discretionary income plans to accommodate new family needs, whether saving for a grandchild's education or covering living expenses for an adult child.

Economic Shifts

The economic environment can be as unpredictable as personal health, with shifts affecting everything from the value of your investments to the cost of living.

Adapting to Economic Conditions:

- **Inflation Adjustments:** Keep a close eye on inflation trends. If the cost of living increases, you may need to adjust your withdrawal rates or shift to investments that offer better protection against inflation, such as Treasury Inflation-Protected Securities (TIPS).

- **Recession Strategies:** During economic downturns, prioritize liquidity and stability. This might mean shifting your portfolio into safer assets or holding off on major discretionary expenditures. While you never want to go all to cash, adjusting your portfolio to be more conservative in economic downturns is okay.

- **Tax Law Changes:** Stay informed about tax legislation that could impact your retirement income. Adjust your investment strategies and retirement withdrawals to optimize tax benefits under new laws. This will be extremely important if you choose to relocate in retirement. If you live in a state with low or no state income taxes and then decide to reallocate to another state with income taxes, you must factor that in.

Retirement life is dynamic, with various changes that can arise, impacting your financial well-being and planning. You can respond effectively by recognizing the common areas where adjustments may be necessary—health changes, family dynamics, and economic shifts—ensuring your retirement plan remains robust and responsive. The key is to stay proactive, regularly review your plan, and remain flexible, allowing you to enjoy your retirement with confidence and peace of mind, regardless of what changes may come.

Adjusting Discretionary Spending

As your financial landscape shifts during retirement, so must your approach to managing discretionary spending. Flexibility is key—not just in how much you spend but also in how you spend it. Adapting your spending habits in response to changes in income or expenses is crucial for maintaining a balanced and joyful retirement.

Strategies for Modulating Discretionary Spending:

- **Prioritize Joy:** Focus on spending that brings the most happiness and fulfillment. This might mean prioritizing travel over hobbies or dining out over high-end entertainment, depending on what brings you the greatest joy.

- **Adjust Spending Levels:** If your income decreases or your essential expenses increase, look for ways to reduce discretionary spending without diminishing your quality of life. This could involve opting for less expensive alternatives or reducing the frequency of certain expenses. This also may naturally happen as you age. Health may take priority over things like travel. This is normal.

- **Income Fluctuations:** When income from investments or part-time work exceeds expectations, consider increasing your discretionary spending proportionately. However, ensure this spending is sustainable and aligned with your long-term financial goals.

Emergency Funds and Contingencies

While we've touched on emergency funds previously, their importance in managing discretionary spending cannot be overstated. A well-maintained emergency fund is a financial buffer, protecting your regular income streams and savings from unexpected expenses.

Building and Maintaining Emergency Funds:

- **Establish a Solid Base:** Aim to set aside enough in your emergency fund to cover at least 3-6 months of living expenses. This provides substantial cushioning against sudden financial needs.

- **Accessibility:** Ensure that your emergency fund is easily accessible. This money should be kept in a liquid form, such as a high-yield savings account or a money market fund, where it can be quickly withdrawn without penalties or significant losses.

- **Regular Reviews:** As part of your periodic financial reviews, assess the adequacy of your emergency fund. If your monthly expenses increase, for example, due to higher medical bills, consider increasing the size of your emergency fund accordingly.

Adjusting discretionary spending in response to life's changes is an essential skill in retirement planning. By implementing flexible spending strategies and maintaining a robust emergency fund, you can ensure that your retirement remains enjoyable and financially secure, regardless of what surprises come your way. This proactive approach allows you to adapt your spending to current financial realities, maximizing your happiness and ensuring continued fulfillment throughout your retirement.

Wrap-Up: Embracing Change In Retirement

As we conclude this chapter on adjusting your retirement plan for life's inevitable changes, remember that flexibility and adaptability are critical to a successful and fulfilling retirement. Your retirement plan is flexible. Still, it is a dynamic blueprint that should evolve with your changing needs, circumstances, and goals.

Key Takeaways

- **Proactive Adjustments:** Manage your retirement plan proactively. Regular reviews and adjustments ensure that your financial strategy aligns with your current life situation and aspirations.

- **Scenario Planning:** Embrace scenario planning as a tool for anticipating and preparing for potential changes. This will help you confidently navigate life's uncertainties and ensure you can adjust your plan effectively when fundamental changes occur.

- **Comprehensive Reviews:** Use tools like the Retirement Plan Adjustment Guide to thoroughly review your financial plan. This systematic approach helps ensure that no aspect of your plan is overlooked and that all elements are harmonized with your current needs.

Moving Forward

As you move forward, treat your retirement plan as a living document that reflects your life's current chapter and anticipates future narratives. The strategies discussed in this chapter are designed to empower you to handle changes gracefully and ensure that your retirement remains as rewarding and secure as intended.

Next Steps

The next chapter will focus on the Growth Pool, the final component of the Sure Horizon Retirement Income Strategy™. This plan will help you combat inflation and provide long-term retirement security.

Your retirement journey is uniquely yours—embrace it fully by staying adaptable, informed, and engaged. Remember, the goal is not just to survive in retirement but to thrive, making the most of every opportunity and challenge that comes your way.

Part III: Securing Your Future With Growth

Chapter 16

Building A Diversified Growth Portfolio

"Every dollar in your growth pool should work harder to keep your future secure."

Regarding retirement planning, diversification isn't just a buzzword thrown around by financial advisors; it's a fundamental principle that can make or break your retirement dreams.

Importance of Diversification

Diversification is the art of not putting all your eggs in one basket. For instance, let's say you have all your savings in one stock. If that stock crashes, you could lose everything. But if you spread your investments across different asset classes and sectors, like stocks, bonds, and real estate, the impact of one area's downturn on your entire portfolio is minimized. Think of it as building a financial safety net: if your stocks stumble, your bonds can keep you afloat; if domestic markets falter, international investments might pick up the slack.

Here's the thing. Retirement is a long game. You need growth investments to stay ahead of inflation and ensure your money lasts. But chasing returns without diversifying can leave you exposed to unnecessary risks. By diversifying smartly, you balance the scales between risk and reward.

Purpose of Growth in Retirement

The purpose of growth investments in retirement is twofold. First, they extend the longevity of your retirement funds. No one wants to outlive their savings, but it's a real possibility with people living longer than ever. Growth investments help ensure your nest egg keeps working for you well into your golden years. Second, they offer a beacon of hope against inflation. Inflation is that sneaky force that chips away at your purchasing power, making today's $ 5 coffee feel like $ 10 a few years later. Without growth investments, your retirement funds could lose their value over time, leaving you struggling to maintain the lifestyle you've worked so hard to enjoy.

Second, they help you combat inflation. Inflation is that sneaky force that chips away at your purchasing power, making today's $5 coffee feel like $10 a few years later. Without growth investments, your retirement funds could lose their value over time, leaving you struggling to maintain the lifestyle you've worked so hard to enjoy.

What to Expect in This Chapter

1. This chapter will explore building a diversified growth portfolio that aligns with your retirement goals and risk tolerance. We'll cover:

2. Strategies for selecting the right mix of investments.

3. How to balance growth potential with risk management.

4. Practical tips for maintaining and adjusting your portfolio over time.

The goal is to give you a roadmap for building a portfolio that grows and is resilient to market turbulence. Let's dive in!

Principals Of Asset Allocation

Asset allocation is one of those financial terms that gets tossed around a lot, but what does it mean? Simply put, it's about dividing your investments among asset categories, such as stocks, bonds, real estate, and cash. Think of it like putting together a balanced diet for your portfolio.

The critical role of asset allocation is to achieve a balanced and effective investment mix that matches your risk tolerance and goals. Here's a quick rundown of the leading asset categories:

- **Stocks** are your portfolio's main engine for growth. They come with higher risk, but the potential for greater returns keeps them attractive. Stocks represent ownership in a company, and their value can fluctuate based on its performance and market conditions. They are considered growth investments because they can potentially increase in value over time.

- **Bonds:** Bonds are your steady-eddy investments. They offer more stability and predictable income than stocks but typically yield lower returns.

- **Real Estate:** Investing in real estate can add another layer of diversification and income through rental yields and property appreciation.

- **Cash and Cash Equivalents:** This includes things like savings accounts and money market funds. They're your safety net for emergencies and provide liquidity.

Now, how you allocate your money among these categories is crucial because it determines both the potential returns and the overall risk of your portfolio.

Tailoring Allocation to Risk Tolerance

Only some people can handle the roller-coaster ride of a high-growth portfolio, especially in retirement when you're no longer adding fresh savings to the mix. But here's the good news: tailoring your asset allocation to your risk tolerance, investment time horizon, and retirement goals is critical to achieving the right balance. This reassures you that you can adapt your investments to changing circumstances, giving you a sense of control and confidence in your financial future.

Understanding Risk Tolerance

Your risk tolerance is how much market fluctuation you can handle without losing sleep. Here's a framework to help you gauge your own:

- **Aggressive Investor:** You're not fazed by market swings and are willing to risk more for potentially higher returns. Your portfolio might consist of 70-80% stocks, with the remainder in bonds or other safer assets.

- **Moderate Investor:** You want growth but also value some stability. Your portfolio might have 50-60% stocks, with the rest in bonds and other assets.

- **Conservative Investor:** Your primary goal is preserving capital; you're willing to sacrifice higher returns for safety. You might have only 30-40% stocks, with most in bonds and other low-risk investments.

Investment Time Horizon and Goals

Your time horizon—the years until you'll need to start drawing on your investments—should also guide your asset allocation. A longer time horizon usually allows for a higher proportion of growth investments because you have more time to ride out market volatility. For example, if you plan to retire in 30 years, you might have a higher allocation to stocks, which have the potential for higher returns over the long term, than if you plan to retire in 5 years.

- **Short-Term (0-5 years):** If you're close to retirement, consider a more conservative allocation with a higher proportion of bonds and cash.

- **Medium-Term (5-15 years):** If retirement is still a few years away, you can afford a mix of growth and conservative assets, leaning more towards stocks.

- **Long-Term (15+ years):** With a long runway ahead, you can afford a more aggressive allocation, emphasizing stocks and real estate.

Putting It All Together

Creating an effective asset allocation is like cooking up a perfect recipe—it takes the right mix of ingredients. Here's a simple framework to follow:

- **Assess Your Risk Tolerance and Time Horizon:** Understand your comfort level with risk and when to start drawing from your portfolio.

- **Define Your Goals:** Identify what you want your investments to achieve. Is it preserving your capital, growing your wealth, or generating income?

- **Allocate Accordingly:** Choose your mix of stocks, bonds, real estate, and cash based on your risk tolerance and goals.

- **Review and Adjust:** Periodically review your portfolio and adjust your allocation as your goals and risk tolerance change.

Understanding asset allocation and tailoring it to your unique situation allows you to build a portfolio that balances growth and stability, giving you the best shot at achieving your retirement goals.

Techniques For Effective Diversification

Diversification is often touted as the "only free lunch in investing," and for good reason. It's your best defense against the market's inherent ups and downs. By spreading your investments across different assets, sectors, and geographies, you manage risk and smooth out the volatility that can rattle even the most seasoned investor.

Managing Risk and Reducing Volatility

Diversification helps minimize the impact of a poor-performing asset or sector. Let's say you have a portfolio heavily weighted in tech stocks. If the tech sector tanks, your entire portfolio takes a hit. However, diversifying across multiple sectors will make that tech slump acceptable because other investments can help cushion the blow. For instance, if you also have investments in healthcare and consumer goods, the losses in those sectors might be offset by gains in the tech sector.

Illustrating Diversification's Impact

Imagine you've invested $10,000 equally in five different asset classes:

- U.S. Stocks

- International Stocks

- Bonds

- Real Estate

- Commodities

Suppose U.S. stocks have a lousy year and drop 10%. In that case, your overall portfolio won't feel that same 10% sting because other investments might balance things out. International stocks could gain 8%, bonds might rise by 3%, and real estate could stay flat, leaving you with a portfolio that weathers the storm.

Diversification Strategies

Now that we understand the benefits, how do we achieve adequate diversification? It's not just about mixing stocks and bonds; it's about understanding the different ways to diversify within and across asset classes.

Diversifying Across Asset Classes

The first layer of diversification is spreading your money across different types of assets.

- **Stocks:** Include a mix of U.S. and international equities.

- **Bonds:** Incorporate various government, corporate, and municipal bonds.

- **Real Estate:** Real estate investment trusts (REITs) provide exposure to property markets.

- **Commodities:** Assets like gold, silver, and oil can protect against inflation.

Diversifying Within Asset Classes

Even within a single asset class like stocks, there are plenty of opportunities to diversify.

- **Sectors:** Spread your equity investments across different sectors like technology, healthcare, finance, consumer goods, and energy. This way, you're not relying too heavily on one industry.

- **Geography:** Invest globally to capture growth from international markets. Developed markets (Europe, Japan) and emerging markets (China, India, Brazil) offer diversification benefits.

- **Market Capitalization:** Mix investments in large-cap, mid-cap, and small-cap companies. Large-cap stocks offer stability, while small-caps often provide higher growth potential.

Diversifying Investment Styles

Investment styles can also provide diversification.

- **Growth vs. Value:** Growth stocks focus on companies expected to increase. In contrast, value stocks are typically undervalued and pay higher dividends.

- **Active vs. Passive Management:** Combine actively managed mutual funds or ETFs with passively managed index funds to balance out performance.

Model Portfolio Example

Here's an example of a diversified portfolio to illustrate how you might spread your investments. This would be typically what we would call a growth oriented portfolio.

- **U.S. Stocks:** 32% (22% Large-Cap, 10% Small/Mid-Cap)

- **International Stocks:** 20% (15% Developed Markets, 5% Emerging Markets)

- **Bonds:** 30% (10% Government, 10% Corporate, 10% High-Yield Corporate)

- **Real Estate:** 10% (REITs)

- **Commodities:** 5% (Gold, Oil)

- **Cash/Cash Equivalents:** 3%

Review and Adjust

Review your portfolio to ensure it remains diversified and aligned with your goals. Market changes can shift your allocation, so rebalancing is crucial to maintain the right mix.

Adequate diversification isn't just about protecting your portfolio from market downturns; it's about creating opportunities for growth while managing risk. By diversifying across and within asset classes, you can build a resilient and poised portfolio for long-term success.

Selecting Investment Vehicles

When building a diversified growth portfolio, choosing suitable investment vehicles is crucial. Here's a quick overview of the primary cars you should consider:

Stocks

Direct ownership of individual stocks can offer high growth potential but comes with higher risk. Owning shares in companies like Apple or Amazon means you're directly tied to their performance—great if they soar, not so great if they stumble.

Mutual Funds

Mutual funds pool money from multiple investors to invest in a diversified portfolio of stocks, bonds, or other assets. They offer professional management and diversification but often have higher fees than other vehicles.

Exchange-traded funds (ETFs)

ETFs are like mutual funds but traded on stock exchanges like individual stocks. They usually have lower fees and can be more tax-efficient. There are ETFs covering everything from broad market indexes to niche sectors.

Real Estate Investments

Real estate can provide steady income through rent and long-term appreciation. Real Estate Investment Trusts (REITs) offer a way to invest in real estate without owning physical property, providing diversification and liquidity.

Bonds

Bonds are debt securities that offer regular interest payments. Government, corporate, and municipal bonds have unique risk and return profiles. Including bonds in your portfolio provides stability and income.

Criteria for Selecting Investments

With so many choices, how do you select the suitable investments for your portfolio? Here are some criteria to guide your decision-making:

- **Historical Performance:** Look at how the investment has performed over time. While past performance doesn't guarantee future results, it can offer insights into how the asset might behave under different market conditions.

- **Fee Structures:** Fees can eat into your returns over time, so pay attention to expense ratios and other costs associated with mutual funds and ETFs. For individual stocks, consider brokerage fees.

- **Liquidity** refers to how quickly and easily an asset can be converted to cash. Stocks and ETFs are highly liquid, while real estate and certain mutual funds might be more challenging to sell quickly.

- **Alignment with Strategy:** Ensure each investment aligns with your portfolio strategy and goals. Growth stocks may offer high returns but can be volatile, while bonds might provide stability but can limit growth potential.

Incorporating New Asset Classes

The investment world constantly evolves, and newer asset classes enter diversified portfolios.

- **Commodities:** Commodities like gold, silver, oil, and agricultural products can hedge against inflation and economic uncertainty. However, they can also be highly volatile and require specialized knowledge to invest effectively.

- **Cryptocurrencies:** Cryptocurrencies like Bitcoin and Ethereum have gained popularity as speculative investments. They offer high potential returns but have significant risk due to their volatility and lack of regulation. If you're considering adding crypto to your portfolio, ensure it's a small allocation and understand the risks involved.

- **Private Equity and Hedge Funds:** Private equity and hedge funds often require high minimum investments and are less liquid but can provide exposure to unique strategies and assets not available through public markets. Some listed Private Equity funds trade on the major exchanges, allowing you to access private equity investments through companies that specialize in making these investments.

Putting It All Together

Here's a practical approach to selecting your investment vehicles:

1. **Start with a Solid Foundation:** To establish diversification and stability, begin with core holdings like broad-market ETFs or mutual funds.

2. **Add Specialized Funds and Stocks:** Based on your risk tolerance and growth goals, layer in sector-specific funds, individual stocks, and bonds.

3. **Incorporate Alternative Assets:** For additional diversification, consider adding REITs, commodities, or cryptocurrencies, but keep allocations small and manageable.

4. **Review and Adjust:** Regularly review your portfolio to ensure your investment vehicles align with your strategy and goals. Adjust as needed based on performance and changing market conditions.

Selecting the suitable investment vehicles is like choosing the right tools for the job. With a clear strategy and the right mix of stocks, funds, and alternative assets, you can build a diversified growth portfolio that's both resilient and positioned for long-term success.

Managing Risk In A Growth Portfolio

Managing risk is vital to a successful growth portfolio. Think of it as your safety net while you're on the high wire of investing. Here's a breakdown of the significant risks to be aware of:

- **Market Risk:** Market risk, or systematic risk, affects every investment somewhat. It's the risk that the whole market will move against you, dragging down even the best-performing stocks. For example, almost everything in your portfolio will likely take a hit if a financial crisis hits.

- **Interest Rate Risk:** Interest rate risk is the danger that changing interest rates will negatively impact your investments. Rising interest rates can cause bond prices to fall, which could be better if you hold long-term bonds. Even stocks can be affected since higher rates often lead to lower corporate profits.

- **Credit Risk:** Credit risk, also known as default risk, is the chance that a bond issuer won't be able to pay interest or repay your principal. You're exposed to this risk if you chase higher yields with corporate bonds. Municipal bonds can also carry credit risk, mainly if issued by financially struggling municipalities.

- **Sector Risk** arises when your portfolio is concentrated too heavily in one sector. For example, if your portfolio is dominated by tech stocks and the tech industry stumbles, your whole portfolio could be in trouble.

- **Liquidity Risk:** Liquidity risk is the danger that you can't sell an investment quickly without taking a hit. Some investments, like small-cap stocks or real estate, can take time to offload soon.

- **Currency Risk:** Currency risk is a concern for international investors. Exchange rate fluctuations can impact foreign investment returns, especially in emerging markets.

Tools for Risk Management

Fortunately, you're not at the mercy of these risks. Here are some tools and techniques to help manage them:

- **Stop-Loss Orders:** Stop-loss orders automatically sell a stock if its price drops to a certain level, protecting you from significant losses. Think of them as your portfolio's airbags. For example, if you bought a stock at $100 and set a stop-loss order at $90, your stock would be sold if the price drops to $90.

- **Position Sizing:** Position sizing is about not putting too many eggs in one basket. Limiting the size of any single investment relative to your overall portfolio can minimize the impact of that investment tank. A common rule of thumb is to keep each stock position to 5-10% of your portfolio.

Hedging Strategies: Hedging is like buying insurance for your portfolio. Here are a couple of common strategies:

- **Put Options:** Buying put options protects your stock positions if the market suddenly dives south. It's like an insurance policy that limits your downside.

- **Inverse ETFs:** These are designed to move in the opposite direction of a particular index, providing some protection when markets fall.

Diversification

We've already covered diversification, but it bears repeating. By spreading your investments across different asset classes, sectors, and regions, you reduce the impact of any single investment going south.

Rebalancing

Regular rebalancing keeps your portfolio aligned with your risk tolerance and goals. If one asset class becomes overweight, sell some gains and rebalance into underweight positions.

Research and Due Diligence

Always do your homework. Thorough research helps you understand the risks involved in any investment. If something sounds too good to be true, it probably is.

Managing risk in growth investing isn't about avoiding risks altogether—that's impossible. It's about understanding the different types of risks and using tools like stop-loss orders, position sizing, and diversification to keep your portfolio on track. By managing these risks smartly, you can confidently navigate the market's ups and downs and stay on the path to long-term success.

Exercise

Exercise: Asset Allocation Review

This exercise will help you assess and refine your current asset allocation to ensure it aligns with your risk tolerance, retirement goals, and time horizon.

Steps

1. **Identify Current Allocation:** Review your portfolio and list your current asset allocation across different categories (stocks, bonds, real estate, etc.).

2. **Evaluate Risk Tolerance:** Refer back to the exercise that we did at the end of chapter 4. Were you an aggressive, moderate, or conservative investor?

   - How would you feel if your portfolio dropped 20% in value tomorrow?

   - How long can you afford to wait for your investments to recover?

3. **Define Retirement Goals and Time Horizon:** Clearly outline your retirement goals (income, travel, legacy, etc.) and the number of years you have left until retirement. As we build your 3 x 3 Retirement Income Strategy™, we will focus on a 5-year horizon to rebuild your discretionary income pool. That is the most important goal when using this strategy.

4. **Adjust Allocation:**

   - If you're too heavily invested in high-risk assets, consider rebalancing towards safer investments.

   - If you're too conservative, consider shifting towards growth investments.

5. **Compare to Target Allocation:** Use the worksheet to compare your current allocation to your ideal target allocation and identify gaps.

Outcome

By completing this exercise, you'll understand how your current asset allocation compares to your desired allocation and be better equipped to make adjustments.

Exercise: Risk Management Strategy Review

This exercise helps you assess your current risk management strategies and identify areas for improvement.

Steps

1. **List Investment Risks:** Write down your portfolio's specific risks (market, interest rate, etc.).

2. **Evaluate Current Risk Management Tools:**

   - Are you using stop-loss orders?

   - Is your position sizing appropriate?

   - Are you diversified enough?

3. **Identify Gaps:** Determine which risks aren't adequately managed and where you could improve.

4. **Develop New Strategies:**

   - Consider adding new tools like options or inverse ETFs.

   - Reevaluate your position sizing and stop-loss orders.

   - Adjust your asset allocation if necessary.

You'll better understand your portfolio's risks and be better equipped to manage them effectively.

Wrap-Up: Building A Diversified Growth Portfolio

In this chapter, we dove into building a diversified growth portfolio that can withstand time and market volatility. Here's a quick recap:

1. **Principles of Asset Allocation:** We discussed how asset allocation is the cornerstone of any investment strategy. It's about dividing your investments among different asset categories, such as stocks, bonds, real estate, and cash, to achieve

a balanced and effective portfolio.

2. **Techniques for Effective Diversification:** Diversification involves mixing stocks and bonds. It's about diversifying across asset classes, sectors, and geographic regions to minimize risk and maximize growth. You can build a resilient portfolio that weathers market storms by spreading your investments wisely.

3. **Selecting Investment Vehicles:** We covered various investment vehicles, from stocks and mutual funds to REITs and cryptocurrencies, and how to choose them based on historical performance, fees, and alignment with your overall strategy.

4. **Risk Management in Growth Investing:** Managing risk is crucial in growth investing. From stop-loss orders to position sizing and diversification, we explored practical tools and techniques to keep your portfolio on track while minimizing potential downsides.

5. **Exercises and Worksheets:** Finally, we provided a series of exercises and worksheets to help you refine your asset allocation, diversify your portfolio, and manage risks effectively. These tools give you actionable steps toward building and maintaining a solid growth portfolio.

Moving Forward

Building a diversified growth portfolio isn't a one-time task; it's a continuous monitoring, adjusting, and refining process. In the next chapter, we'll explore how to monitor and adjust your growth pool over time to ensure it continues delivering the returns you need for a secure and prosperous retirement.

We'll cover practical strategies for rebalancing, keeping your portfolio aligned with your goals, and responding to market changes smartly. So, let's keep moving toward financial security and success in retirement!

Chapter 17

Monitoring And Adjusting Your Growth Pool

"Rebalancing isn't just an action—it's a strategy to keep your retirement goals on track."

Managing your retirement portfolio is like tending to a garden—it needs your regular care, attention, and the occasional pruning to keep it healthy and fruitful. Your Growth Pool is no different. While building a diversified and growth-oriented portfolio is essential, the real magic happens with your ongoing management.

When we look at your overall Retirement Income Strategy, the Growth Pool is where you will spend most of your portfolio management time. When you build your plan, the decisions on the Essential Income Pool are typically only done once or twice over your entire retirement. The discretionary pool will usually only be worked with every five years, so there is little to do.

Importance of Active Management

Actively managing your Growth Pool is not just a necessity but also a source of empowerment. It's about maintaining a steady hand, aligning your portfolio with your risk tolerance and financial objectives, and feeling in control of your retirement goals.

Effective portfolio management involves regular monitoring and timely adjustments. Here's why:

- **Market Fluctuations:** Markets change, and so do investment opportunities.

Monitoring your portfolio helps you capitalize on new trends and minimize risks.

- **Life Changes:** Your financial goals may shift as your life circumstances evolve. Your portfolio should reflect those changes involving a new grandchild or a health concern.

- **Economic Environment:** Inflation, interest rates, and tax policies can impact your portfolio's performance. Staying on top of these changes allows you to adjust accordingly.

Setting Expectations

Setting realistic expectations for your Growth Pool's performance is not just important. It's crucial. Here's what that means:

- **Understand Market Volatility:** Growth investments are inherently volatile. A well-diversified portfolio can help smooth the ride but won't eliminate market downturns. Be prepared for short-term ups and downs while keeping your long-term goals in mind.

- **Align with Broader Financial Goals:** Your Growth Pool should align with your broader financial goals and retirement timeline. Plan accordingly if you need to replenish your Discretionary Income Fund in five years. If you're aiming to build a legacy, think beyond your lifetime.

- **Stay Flexible:** The best-laid plans can change, and that's okay. Being flexible is not a weakness but a strength. If market conditions shift or your risk tolerance changes, be ready to adjust your Growth Pool without overreacting. In this chapter, we'll cover the following:

- **Setting Performance Benchmarks:** How to measure your portfolio's performance against meaningful benchmarks.

- **Regular Monitoring Strategies:** Practical tips for staying on top of your portfolio's health.

- **Rebalancing Your Portfolio:** When and how to rebalance your portfolio to maintain your target allocation.

- **Responding to Major Market Changes:** Strategies for adjusting your portfolio in response to significant market shifts.

By the end of this chapter, you'll understand how to monitor and adjust your Growth Pool over time to ensure it continues to deliver the returns you need for a comfortable and secure retirement.

Monitoring The Growth Pool

Let's face it, managing your portfolio isn't just a "set it and forget it" proposition. You've got to keep an eye on the prize and ensure your Growth Pool delivers the returns you need to stay on course. Here's how to do just that.

Performance Tracking

When tracking performance, don't rely on your brokerage account's "You've gained/lost X%" report. Dig deeper.

One of the most consequential parts of your Growth Pool will be its total return. Your total return includes capital gains, dividends, and interest. It's the real bottom line of how your investments are performing. The total return is calculated using the following formula:

(Ending Value-Beginning Value) + Dividends + Interest/Beginning Value

You want to see how your Growth Pool is genuinely doing, especially compared to a standard benchmark like the S&P 500, an index of the 500 most extensive publicly traded stocks in the United States. Benchmarks, like the S&P 500, help you see if your Growth Pool is growing or if you're treading water. Compare your portfolio to indices that match your asset allocation. Here are some standard benchmarks:

- U.S. Stocks: S&P 500, Russell 2000

- International Stocks: MSCI EAFE, MSCI Emerging Markets

- Bonds: Bloomberg Barclays U.S. Aggregate Bond Index

- Real Estate: FTSE NAREIT All Equity REIT Index

Blend Your Benchmarks

Create a blended benchmark that matches your asset allocation. For example, if your Growth Pool is 60% U.S. stocks, 30% bonds, and 10% international stocks, your blended benchmark could include:

- S&P 500 Index: 60%

- Bloomberg Barclays U.S. Aggregate Bond Index: 30%

- MSCI EAFE Index: 10%

Expense Ratios

Don't let high fees drain your returns. Keep an eye on expense ratios for mutual funds and ETFs, and factor in trading fees for individual stocks. While not something you need to look at every quarter, this should be part of your annual portfolio review and your evaluation of new investments. Even a 1% difference in fees can significantly impact your returns.

Periodic Reviews

Quarterly Reviews

Think of these as regular maintenance on your car. A quick quarterly review can help you catch significant changes before they become bigger problems:

- Is the Portfolio Aligned?:

- Is your portfolio still in line with your target allocation?

- Any Underperformers?:

- Are any specific investments significantly underperforming?

Semi-Annual Reviews

Go a little deeper with a semi-annual review to ensure everything is in tip-top shape:

- How does your Growth Pool compare to your chosen benchmarks?

- Are there noticeable trends in returns or volatility?

- Do you need to rebalance your portfolio to stay on track?

Annual Reviews

The annual review is where you get down to brass tacks and thoroughly assess your portfolio's health. This is also the time to evaluate changes in your life, market, and economic shifts and look at Tax Optimization.

- Have your goals or circumstances changed due to retirement, health, or family?

- How have inflation, interest rates, or tax policies affected your portfolio?

- Are you minimizing taxes effectively through tax-advantaged accounts and strategies?

- Do you have the opportunity to do any tax loss harvesting, sell things that are down for the capital loss, and replace them with something similar?

During Volatile Markets or Life Changes

Sometimes, life happens, or the market decides to play hardball. In those cases, you should review your Growth Pool more frequently; however, try to avoid knee-jerk reactions by looking at a period that is too short. For example, in the portfolios we manage for clients at my firm, we have a model that we adjust monthly (the first trading day of the month). We are professionals, so it is our job to do this, but you must have a regular schedule to rebalance your accounts. I recommend quarterly, at least.

Monitoring your Growth Pool regularly is like steering a ship—you must keep an eye on the horizon while ensuring the engine room is in top shape. By tracking key metrics, setting relevant benchmarks, and reviewing performance at the proper intervals, you'll stay on course for a secure and prosperous retirement.

The following section will explore how to rebalance your portfolio to maintain your target asset allocation and keep your Growth Pool on track.

Rebalancing Your Portfolio

Your Growth Pool is like a well-tuned engine, but even the best engines need regular maintenance to keep them running smoothly. That's where rebalancing comes in. It's not just a chore—it's crucial to maintaining your portfolio's risk-return profile. Hence, it matches your current needs and goals.

Purpose of Rebalancing

Rebalancing ensures that your portfolio remains aligned with your original investment strategy, which was designed based on your risk tolerance, time horizon, and financial goals.

Over time, some investments will outperform while others underperform, throwing your portfolio's balance out of whack. For example, if stocks have a strong year, their proportion in your portfolio may increase significantly, leaving you overexposed to market risk.

Rebalancing ensures that your portfolio sticks to the initial investment strategy you laid out. With it, your portfolio could stay on track with your target allocation.

Rebalancing encourages you to sell appreciated assets and buy underperforming ones by selling high and low, which is the essence of successful investing.

Rebalancing Strategies

Here are a few common strategies to help you rebalance your portfolio effectively:

1. **Calendar Rebalancing:** Rebalance your portfolio at fixed intervals, regardless of market conditions. Popular intervals include quarterly, semi-annually, or annually.

2. **Percentage-Range Rebalancing:** Rebalance when asset classes deviate from

their target allocation by a predetermined percentage. For example, imagine your target allocation is 60% stocks, 30% bonds, and 10% real estate. You set a +/- 5% range for each asset class. If stocks grow to 66% of the portfolio (above the 65% threshold), sell some stocks to rebalance back to 60%.

Rebalancing is all about keeping your Growth Pool in line with your risk tolerance and investment strategy. Whether you prefer calendar rebalancing, percentage-range rebalancing, or threshold rebalancing, the goal is to maintain a healthy balance that aligns with your retirement goals.

The following section will explore how to respond to significant market changes and ensure your Growth Pool remains resilient in volatile conditions.

Adjusting For Changes

Even the best-laid plans can go off track when life throws a curveball. Whether the economy nosediving or a sudden change in your circumstances, your Growth Pool must stay nimble to keep delivering on your retirement goals.

Responding to Economic Shifts

The nature of our 5-year strategy for the Growth Pool tends to mute some of the volatility that occurs in the market. Market downturns and economic booms are part and parcel of investing. That does not mean that you just let things go in the case of a market downturn. One of the core tenants of my investing style is the "Stock Market Cash Trigger" that I learned from my mentor David Alan Carter in his excellent book, *STOCK MARKET CASH TRIGGER: Learn A Simple Technique That Tells You When To Go To Cash* (Carter, David Alan. *Stock Market Cash Trigger*. Echo West Publishing, April 2018). In David's book, he espouses a simple trading formula that uses the 200-day moving average of the S&P 500 index to determine if your portfolio should be Risk on or Risk off each month. You should be at risk if the index is above 200 days. You should be at risk if the index exceeds the 200-day moving average. While our system is more sophisticated from that strategy, that basic premise has served our clients well throughout the craziness and uncertainty that the markets can deliver.

Shifting to More Stable Assets During Market Downturns

When the economy starts to wobble and the market plunges, it's tempting to panic and sell everything. This is almost always the worst option. Instead, consider shifting part of your Growth Pool to more stable assets.

That means reducing your exposure to stocks a bit and increasing exposure to bonds and cash. Using the *Stock Market Cash Trigger* strategy, David Carter espouses in his book might also be more dramatic.

Adapting to Personal Circumstances

Life has a funny way of not going according to plan, especially regarding personal circumstances. Whether it's a health issue, a change in retirement plans, or a sudden family need, here's how to keep your Growth Pool on track.

Health Issues or Medical Expenses

If unexpected health issues arise, your financial priorities need to shift.

- **Increase Emergency Funds:** With the additional strain on your finances, pulling some risks off the table can make sense. Making sure that you increase your emergency fund to at least 6 months of your basic needs (above what you have coming in from guaranteed income) is prudent.

- **Consider Annuities:** While a short-term financial strain from health can be handled by increasing your Emergency Fund, longer-term health issues might mean a longer-term strain on your income. At these times, it can be wise to shift some of your growth pool and possibly redirect some of your discretionary pool to an additional Income Annuity to cover this extra expense.

- **Reduce High-Risk Investments:** Adjusting your asset allocation to be a bit more conservative (e.g., reducing stocks and adding bonds and cash) can also be prudent to protect your capital in case you need more.

Changes in Retirement Plans

Sometimes, retirement doesn't go exactly as planned, and that's okay. Here's how to adjust your Growth Pool. Many people worldwide decided to retire a little earlier than scheduled during the global pandemic. However, with a dramatic increase in living costs over the last 4 years, some people realize that they may need to adjust their plans to prolong their retirement savings. These shifts have led to some people going back to work. Working part-time somewhere you enjoy can prolong your retirement assets. As a business owner, we really need you right now.

Another common thing happening today is people with larger homes downsizing. When working with clients, we have a significant conversation about when they are going into retirement. Do you need the 4 bedroom house if only two of you are available? Do you need to live close to a major city now that you are no longer commuting?

Many clients will say that they want the larger house for when family visits (how many times per year does this occur). How about going to them instead of them coming to you?

The decisions you make around how to "Right Size" your life can help to reduce the drain on your retirement income.

Adjusting your Growth Pool to economic shifts and personal changes is all about staying flexible and prepared. Whether you move to defensive assets during downturns or increase equity exposure in bull markets, keeping your portfolio nimble ensures you stay on course despite the bumps in the road.

Exercises

Worksheet: Growth Pool Monitoring Log

Purpose

The Growth Pool Monitoring Log helps you monitor your portfolio's performance and track rebalancing actions. It's like a diary for your investments, helping you see the bigger picture and make informed adjustments. Here is how I would suggest that you layout the worksheet:

Insert Growth Pool Monitoring Log Image

Usage Guide:

- **Fill in the date and total value of the Growth Pool regularly, especially after significant market movements or personal events.**

- **Record any rebalancing actions taken, including the specifics of what was bought or sold, and why these actions were necessary.**

- **Note any major economic changes that could impact your investments and describe their immediate impact on your Growth Pool.**

- **Update any personal life changes that could affect your financial strategy or needs, such as retirement or receiving a large inheritance.**

- **Use the Notes section for general observations or thoughts about the investment environment or your personal strategy.**

- **Plan for future actions based on the current state of your investments and anticipated changes in your life or the economy.**

Chapter Exercise: Rebalancing Scenario Analysis

Purpose

The Rebalancing Scenario Analysis exercise lets you practice rebalancing a hypothetical portfolio based on different scenarios. It's a great way to understand when and how to apply various rebalancing strategies without risking your investments.

Scenario Setup

Initial Allocation:

- Stocks: 60%

- Bonds: 30%

- Real Estate: 10%

Benchmarks:

- Stocks: S&P 500

- Bonds: Bloomberg Barclays U.S. Aggregate Bond Index

- Real Estate: FTSE NAREIT All Equity REITs Index

Scenarios to Practice

Scenario 1: Market Boom

The stock market rallies, increasing the portfolio's allocation to 75%. Real estate performs moderately well, increasing to 12%. Bonds drop to 13%.

How would you rebalance this portfolio to fit the model?

Scenario 2: Market Downturn

The stock market plunges, reducing the stock allocation to 45%.

Bonds increase to 45%.

Real estate remains stable at 10%.

How would you rebalance this scenario?

Scenario 3: Personal Change

You've decided to retire early and need to reduce portfolio risk.

Shift to a more conservative allocation with a 40% stocks, 50% bonds, and 10% real estate target. How would you do this rebalance?

How to Complete the Exercise

1. **Assess Current Allocation:** Calculate your current asset allocation under each scenario.

2. **Determine Rebalancing Needs:** Identify which assets are over or under-weighted based on your target allocation.

3. **Choose a Rebalancing Strategy:** Choose a rebalancing strategy (calendar, percentage range, or threshold) and apply it to each scenario.

4. **Implement Changes:** Adjust the hypothetical portfolio to reflect your chosen rebalancing strategy.

5. **Evaluate Impact:** Analyze how the rebalanced portfolio performs compared to the initial allocation.

Outcome

By completing this exercise, you'll better understand how different rebalancing strategies work in practice and how to effectively apply them to your Growth Pool.

These exercises and worksheets will help you monitor your Growth Pool more effectively and make smarter rebalancing decisions. By staying on top of your portfolio's performance and practicing different rebalancing scenarios, you'll be well-prepared to align your Growth Pool with your retirement goals.

Wrap-Up: Long-Term Success Through Active Management

Managing your Growth Pool isn't just a one-time effort—it requires ongoing attention and adjustment, much like maintaining a vibrant garden. Here's why it's crucial:

Imagine your investment portfolio as a garden. Initially, you plant various seeds (investments) that you hope will flourish. However, as in any garden, some plants might grow too vigorously, overshadowing others, while others might not thrive. This necessitates a few key gardening actions: weeding out the underperformers to prevent them from draining resources, trimming back the overachievers to maintain balance, and fertilizing—adding resources to areas that need a boost to continue thriving.

Your Growth Pool needs similar care:

- **Track Performance:** Regularly review metrics like total return, volatility, and how your investments compare to benchmarks. This helps you understand which investments are thriving and which are not.

- **Set Realistic Expectations:** Recognize that markets fluctuate; growth isn't always linear. Anticipate variations in performance.

- **Stay Aligned:** Continually ensure that your investments support your broader retirement goals. They should evolve as your objectives and needs do.

- **Rebalance Regularly:** Establish a rebalancing strategy—whether at set time intervals, when assets deviate from target allocations by a certain percentage, or when the overall risk level crosses a predefined threshold—and adhere to it diligently.

- **Respond to Changes:** Be proactive in adapting to market changes and shifts in your personal retirement plans. If the market takes a downturn or if your financial goals change, adjust your strategy to remain on target.

- **Adapt to Life Events:** Personal events like health changes or family milestones can impact your financial needs and goals. Be prepared to adjust your Growth Pool to address these changes.

As we move forward, we'll explore how to strategically and tax-efficiently replenish your Discretionary Income Fund from your Growth Pool. This ensures that you can enjoy your retirement comfortably while maintaining the health of your investments. Stay engaged and proactive—the key to a successful financial future.

Chapter 18

Using the Growth Pool To Replenish Your Discretionary Pool

"Every retirement plan starts with a single goal: securing your future. Build it brick by brick."

Let's face it, the joys of retirement aren't just about covering your essential expenses—they're also about the fun stuff: travel, dining out, hobbies, and spoiling the grandkids. That's where your Discretionary Income Fund comes into play. But to keep the good times rolling, you must ensure that your Discretionary Income Bond Ladder remains fully funded.

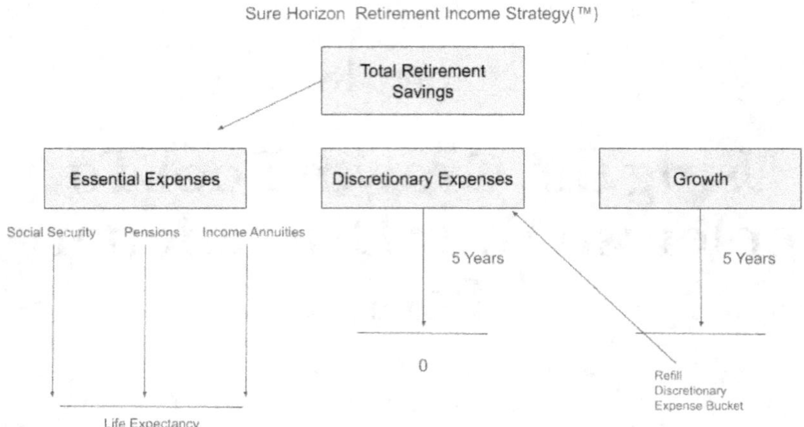

Purpose of Replenishment

Every five years, your Discretionary Income Bond Ladder will need a fresh infusion from your Growth Pool. Think of it like refilling a gas tank on a road trip. If you don't top it off, you won't have enough fuel to enjoy the ride.

Regular replenishment is not just a financial task. It's a key to maintaining your envisioned retirement lifestyle. Keeping your Discretionary Fund topped up allows you to enjoy your discretionary spending without compromising your essential needs or long-term growth. This approach also brings more certainty and less guesswork to your retirement journey.

Balancing Withdrawal and Growth

Managing your portfolio in retirement is a delicate balance. You need to carefully plan your periodic withdrawals to ensure they align with the ongoing growth of your portfolio. Withdraw too much, and you risk the long-term growth of your investments. Withdraw too little, and you may not fully enjoy the retirement you've worked hard for. Striking this balance is crucial for your financial future.

In this chapter, we'll cover:

- **Timing the Replenishment:** How to decide when and how often to replenish your Discretionary Fund.

- **Calculating Withdrawal Amounts:** How much can you withdraw from your

Growth Pool to cover discretionary spending?

- **Tax-Efficient Withdrawals:** Strategies to minimize taxes on your withdrawals.

- **Scenario Analysis:** Practical examples to illustrate how to replenish your Discretionary Fund effectively.

So, with your financial advisor by your side, let's discuss how to keep your Discretionary Income Fund fueled for your retirement adventures! Their expertise and guidance will be invaluable as you navigate these strategies.

Tax Implications Of Withdrawals

Replenishing your Discretionary Income Fund is a financial necessity, but doing it tax-efficiently is equally important. Without a clear understanding of tax implications, you might pay more taxes than necessary, affecting your overall retirement income. Being well-informed and making smart financial decisions is crucial to protect your hard-earned money.

Understanding Tax Impacts

Before diving into strategies, let's clarify the tax implications of withdrawing from different accounts.

Taxable Accounts

You'll incur capital gains taxes if you sell investments in a taxable account for a profit. Investments held for less than a year are taxed at your ordinary income tax rate, called Short-Term Capital Gains. Investments held for over a year are taxed at a lower rate (0%, 15%, or 20%, depending on your income) and are called Long-Term Capital Gains.

Tax-Deferred Accounts

The primary types of investments in this category are Traditional IRAs and 401ks. Withdrawals from these accounts are taxed as ordinary income. You can begin withdrawing from these accounts without penalty starting at age 59 1/2. Once you reach age 73 (for those born after 1950), you must begin taking RMDs (Required Minimum Distributions) from tax-deferred accounts, and these withdrawals will be fully taxable.

Tax-Free Accounts

Withdrawals from Roth IRAs and Roth 401ks are tax-free, provided the account has been open for at least five years, and you're 59½ or older.

Qualified medical expenses can be paid tax-free from HSAs (Health Savings Accounts), making them helpful in covering healthcare costs in retirement.

Strategies for Minimizing Taxes

As you look at where you will withdraw money to recharge your Discretionary Pool, you will want to consider taxes as you plan your withdrawals. To avoid getting bumped into a higher tax bracket, plan your withdrawals strategically:

- **Spread Large Withdrawals:** If you need to withdraw a significant amount, consider spreading it over multiple years to prevent crossing into a higher bracket.

- **Bracket Management:** Understand the thresholds for each tax bracket and plan your withdrawals to stay within the desired range.

Harvesting Capital Gains and Losses

Capital gains and losses can significantly impact your tax bill. Here's how to leverage them:

- **Harvest Losses:** Sell underperforming investments to realize losses that can offset gains and reduce your taxable income.

- **Long-Term Gains:** Focus on long-term capital gains to benefit from lower tax rates.

Required Minimum Distributions (RMDs)

If you're required to take RMDs, here's how to handle them smartly:

- **Plan Early:** Start planning for RMDs a few years before they become mandatory to avoid large taxable distributions.

- **Charitable Donations:** Consider a Qualified Charitable Distribution (QCD) to donate directly to charity from your IRA, which can satisfy your RMD requirement without increasing your taxable income.

Keeping Your Discretionary Pool Inside Your Tax-Advantaged Account

If most of your money is in a tax-advantaged account such as a Traditional IRA, you can simply buy your bond ladder inside that account. As the bonds mature, you will be able to draw that money out in five segments over five years, keeping your overall taxes down.

Scenario Example

Scenario: Frank is 72 years old and has a mix of taxable accounts, a traditional IRA, and a Roth IRA. He needs $100,000 from his investments to recharge his Discretionary Income Pool, which amounts to $20,000 annually. Frank has $250,000 in his Roth IRA, $500,000 in an IRA that came from a 401k at work, and $300,000 in a Taxable Account.

Working with his Financial Advisor, Frank makes the following withdrawals from his accounts:

- **Roth IRA:** Frank decides to withdraw $50,000 from his Roth, resulting in no tax liability for these funds.

- **Traditional IRA:** This is Frank's first year having to take an RMD from this account, and he decides to take the minimum that he can out of it this year. His RMD for the first year is $18,248, which is fully taxable.

- **Taxable Account:** Frank decides to take the remaining money from his taxable account for $31,752. Most of the assets in this account are company stock from Frank's old company and are on a low basis (the amount they were acquired over time). Due to some market volatility this year, Frank and his advisor have been harvesting tax losses from his account. Those tax losses have amounted to $10,500 by year-end. The end result for Frank is a capital gain of $21,252, which keeps him at the 0% capital gains tax rate for this year.

Frank could use innovative withdrawal strategies to recharge his discretionary income pool by $100,000 with minimal tax impact. His Roth IRA withdrawal had zero tax impact, and the RMD from Traditional IRA was taxable but minimally so. The withdrawal from his taxable account of $31,752 minus the $10,500 capital loss was not taxed as income since it was a long-term capital gain (owned over a year). This withdrawal's "taxable" amount was a capital gain of $21,252. This amount falls into the 0% band of capital gains, so Frank will own no tax on this money.

This combination of withdrawals amounted to only $18,248 being taxed as income for the year. Frank's other income (Social Security and Annuity Income) kept him in the 15% tax bracket. Hence, Franks RMD cost him $2737 in taxes for the year.

The real advantage for Frank is that over the next five years, the income from his Discretionary Income Pool will not generate any capital gains and only minimal interest, resulting in an extremely tax-efficient "Fun Money" pool. As a result, Frank and his advisor plan to do a series of Roth conversions over the next five years, which will move even more money from his Traditional IRA into the Roth IRA with minimal tax loss.

Tax-efficient withdrawals can save you thousands of dollars throughout your retirement. By understanding the tax implications of different accounts and leveraging strategies like Roth IRA withdrawals and tax bracket management, you'll keep more of your money working for you.

Rebalancing After Withdrawals

When you withdraw funds to replenish your Discretionary Income Fund, it's crucial to rebalance your portfolio afterward to ensure it remains aligned with your long-term goals. Let's explore how post-withdrawal rebalancing keeps your portfolio on track.

Post-Withdrawal Rebalancing

After a significant withdrawal, your portfolio balance might be out of whack, and you will need to reallocate your assets. One of the advantages of the 3 x 3 Retirement Income Strategy™ is that we are still determining our portfolio strategy based on Risk tolerance.

We can calculate what the portfolio needs to make over the next five years so we can invest accordingly.

If our portfolio needs 4% or less, we can take a little risk to succeed. However, if our need is greater at 7-8%, we will have to take more risk to achieve that.

Continual Monitoring

As discussed in the previous chapter, rebalancing isn't a one-time fix. You must continually monitor your portfolio's performance and composition to adapt to market shifts or changes in your financial goals. The advantage is that you know your time horizon (five years) and what your portfolio needs to achieve.

Rebalancing after withdrawals is essential to keeping your Growth Pool aligned with your long-term financial goals. By continually monitoring your portfolio's performance and composition, you'll stay one step ahead of market shifts and life changes.

What happens If The Markets Are Down?

If you reach the end of your 5-year period and your portfolio average is down, you can do a couple of things.

1. **If Things Are Significantly Down:** In this situation, you might not want to fund your discretionary income pool fully. Only take a year's worth of money from your Growth Pool to use as "Fun Money," leaving the remaining four years working in the Growth Pool, allowing it to recover.

2. **If The Growth Pool Slightly Down:** Once again, I would take one or two years out of the Growth Pool at that time and let the rest continue to recover, reevaluating the following year.

3. **If the Growth Pool is Flat or Didn't Perform as Expected,** I would probably fully recharge the 5-year Discretionary Income Pool.

These scenarios are just examples. You should evaluate them based on your situation and make the most comfortable decision. This allows you to take advantage of market highs while limiting your exposure to portfolio drops.

Wrap-Up: Sustaining Retirement Enjoyment

Retirement isn't just about covering the basics; it's about embracing the freedom to live your best life—whether that means traveling the world, picking up new hobbies, or spending quality time with family. Managing and replenishing your Discretionary Income Fund is crucial to sustain that lifestyle.

By carefully planning your withdrawals, timing them efficiently, and minimizing your tax burden, you'll keep the good times rolling without risking your long-term financial health.

Key Takeaways

- **Regular Replenishment:** Keep your Discretionary Income Fund topped up every five years.

- **Timing is Everything:** Withdraw during market highs and avoid selling assets at a loss.

- **Tax Efficiency:** Use Roth IRAs, tax-loss harvesting, and careful withdrawal ordering to minimize taxes.

Call to Action

Here's your game plan to keep the fun in retirement:

1. **Set Regular Review Dates:** Schedule regular review dates for your withdrawal strategy—quarterly, semi-annually, or annually.

2. **Stay Informed on Tax Law Changes:** Tax laws can change quickly, so stay updated on the latest rules that may impact your withdrawals.

3. **Consult a Financial Advisor:** Work with a financial advisor to ensure your strategy remains optimal. They can provide tailored advice based on your unique situation.

With these strategies in place, you'll keep your Discretionary Income Fund well-fueled, ensuring you can enjoy retirement fully.

In the next chapter, we'll explore real-life case studies and success stories to bring these strategies to life and show you how others have successfully navigated their retirement journeys.

Part IV: Bringing It All Together

Chapter 19

Case Studies And Success Stories

"The Sure Horizon Retirement Income Strategy™ is more than a financial plan—it's your blueprint for a secure and prosperous retirement."

We've covered the theory behind the Sure Horizon Retirement Income Strategy™, explored its key strategies, and dived deep into the tactics for building a secure retirement. Now, let's bring these concepts to life with real-world examples.

In the following pages, you'll find stories of people who successfully navigated their retirement journeys using our strategies. From securing their Essential Income to managing their Growth Pools, these case studies will give you a firsthand look at applying these principles in your retirement planning.

Scenario 1: Planning at Mid-Career

Meet Paul Rogers, a mid-career professional who got a wake-up call about his retirement planning when he turned 55. For most of his career, he focused on providing for his family and covering day-to-day expenses rather than planning for his golden years. Paul's wife, Trina, was a stay-at-home mom for the entire time their kids were home. Now that their final child has left the house, she works outside the home again.

The details of Paul and Trina's situation:

- **Ages:** Both 55

- **Professions:** Sales Director and Executive Assistant

- **Annual Income:** $140,000

- **Initial Retirement Savings:** $250,000

- **Goal:** Retire at 65 with enough guaranteed income to cover essential expenses and a sufficient discretionary fund.

Challenges:

- **High Living Expenses:** Mortgage and college tuition costs have impacted their savings rate for most of their working years.

- **Portfolio Imbalance:** Heavy reliance on stocks with no guaranteed income sources.

Trigger for Change

Paul and Trina's turning point came during a financial review with a new advisor, Nathan. Nathan pointed out that Paul and Trina's current portfolio couldn't comfortably cover their living expenses in retirement. Additionally, while their heavy reliance on stocks could provide needed growth over the final 10 working years, it offered no protection in a market downturn. With only 10 years left until retirement, Paul and Trina realized they needed to act quickly.

Strategy Implemented

After a comprehensive review, with Nathan's help, Paul and Trina implemented the following strategies using the 3 x 3 Retirement Income Strategy™.

1. Essential Income

- **Delay Retirement:** They delayed their retirement to age 67 for a few more savings years.

- **Indexed Deferred Annuity:** They shifted $150,000 of their assets from two old 401ks that Paul and Trina had with former employers to an Indexed Deferred Annuity. These annuities are designed to provide $1975 monthly at age 67 when the income stream is turned on. Paul and Trina will each make maximum ROTH IRA contributions (currently $7500 each with catch-up contributions) for the next 17 years until they retire.

- **Social Security Optimization: With** Nathan's help, they will delay Social Security benefits until age 70 to maximize monthly payouts. This will represent about a 23% increase in their payouts for waiting. Their social security calculation was based on Trina taking the option of half of Paul's Social Security. Over the next 17 years, her income may create a larger payout at retirement based on her earnings, which she would elect at that time.

2. Discretionary Income

Since discretionary Income can be covered from excess earnings at this point, the following was done to prepare for future discretionary income needs:

- **Dividend Portfolio:** Paul and Trina decided to rebalance a portion of their portfolio to include a diversified set of high-yield dividend stocks. This will provide diversification and stability that can later be converted into a discretionary income pool as they approach retirement.

3. Growth Pool

- **Maximized 401(k) Contributions:** With Trina back at work, they will increase 401(k) contributions to the maximum allowable limit of $30,500 per year (including catch-up contributions) for Paul. Trina will contribute to her 401k up to the match limit from her company. These contributions will be made into the ROTH 401k options available through work, which will create a pool of tax-free Income to reduce taxes in retirement. Company matching will be made pretax and taxable when Paul and Trina retire. However, they consider doing ROTH conversions inside their 401k to eliminate taxes later in life.

- **Asset Allocation Adjustments:** Nathan shifted from a 90% growth equity-heavy portfolio to a more moderate allocation, which included the following:

  - Growth Equities: 25%

  - Dividend Equities Discussed Above 25%

  - Real Estate REITs: 25%

  - Diversified Bonds including High Yield: 15%

  - Diversified International Stocks: 10%

- **Roth IRA Contributions:** Nathan helped Paul and Trina open Roth IRAs in the same Indexed Deferred Annuities they had created in the Essential Income bucket, which will be converted to additional essential Income at retirement. They will contribute the maximum for the next 17 years ($7,500 per year each, including catch-up contributions).

- **Consistent Rebalancing:** Nathan will help them rebalance their portfolio annually to maintain the new allocation.

Outcome

By age 67, Paul and Trina will have significantly improved their financial outlook, retiring with over $2,250,000 in their accounts. Here's how their retirement income broke down:

1. Essential Income

- **Deferred Income Annuities** (Annuitized for Lifetime Income with a maximum Guarantee Period (of approximately 22 years) provide $1,975 per month for life taxable income and $2063 per month in Tax-Free Income from the ROTH Annuities for life.

- **Social Security:** Monthly benefits of $2,500 for Paul and $1750 for Trina starting at age 70.

- 401k Withdrawals of $2500 monthly for Paul and $1750 per Trina from 67-70 as a bridge to Social Security.

Paul and Trina's Guaranteed Income from Annuities and Social Security amounts to $8288 per month or $99,456 per year. Due to the significant amount of Tax-Free Income they receive, their Social Security income is not taxed, leaving them with most of their Income spendable each month.

2. Discretionary Income

- **Bond Ladder:** A year before retirement, Nathan helped Paul and Trina do in-service rollovers from their 401k plans (typically allowed after age 59.5), placing the money in Roth IRA accounts (they had converted all their pretax funds to ROTH 401ks). At that point, Nathan set up a 5-year bond ladder for Paul and Trina using $200,000 of their portfolio. This money would provide them $40,000 per year of tax-free Income as each bond matures plus interest. In 5 years, when this pool exhausts itself, they will rebuild a new bond ladder from funds in their growth pool.

3. Growth Pool

Roger's essential income needs are taken care of through guaranteed Indemnities and social security, and their discretionary income is taken care of with withdrawals from their bond ladder; they now have a stable and sustainable income. The remaining assets for the Rogers (roughly $800,000) can be invested as a Growth Pool for them with 5 more years before they need to refund their Discretionary Pool.

- **Sustainable withdraws:** With a starting value of $800,000 and 5 years for the growth pool to grow back to its original $1,000,000, a simple financial calculation reveals that Paul and Trina need to average 4.56% growth over the next 5 years to be able to refund their Discretionary Pool and do the same thing over again. This is a reachable goal for an undisturbed growth portfolio over 5 years.

- **Annual Rebalances:** Working with Nathan, Rogers has continued to rebalance its growth portfolio each year and has kept its asset allocation the same. This will likely stay the same unless they have a greater need for income, in which case they might need to become more conservative.

Lessons Learned

Paul and Trina's story provides valuable lessons for mid-career professionals starting late. While you might not be in the position to put away as much money as the Rogers, their principles do not change:

- **Prioritize Guaranteed Income:** Incorporate annuities or pensions to secure essential expenses and optimize your Social Security decisions.

- **Maximize Tax-Advantaged Accounts:** Rogers maximized its contributions to 401ks and IRAs and optimized them by making ROTH contributions to both. They maximized their contributions by making catch-up contributions that they were able to make since they were over the age of 50.

- **Rebalance for Balance:** Shift away from aggressive growth equity-heavy portfolios and include bonds and REITs for stability.

- **Add Dividend Stocks:** Eliminating some risky growth assets and reallocating those funds to dividend-producing stocks helped stabilize their portfolio and prepare them for Discretionary Income when it was time.

Key Takeaways

Paul and Trina's story shows that even if you start late, it's always possible to turn things around and secure a comfortable retirement. In the following case study, we'll meet Linda, a high-earning executive who needed to balance significant assets while planning for early retirement.

Scenario 2: Linda's Late Start

Meet Linda Stringer, a late starter who only began severe retirement planning at age 60. A successful real estate agent for over 30 years and a divorcee, she was accustomed to living comfortably but never prioritized retirement savings. She now realized she could only retire if she did something immediately.

Here are the details of Linda's situation:

- **Age:** 60

- **Profession:** Real Estate Agent

- **Annual Income:** $150,000

- **Initial Retirement Savings:** $130,000

- **Goal:** Retire at 68 with a secure retirement income to cover essential expenses and enjoy discretionary activities.

Challenges:

- **Short-Time Horizon:** Only 8 years until planned retirement.

- **High Living Expenses:** Mortgage, business costs, and lifestyle spending reduced her saving ability.

Strategy Implemented

At age 60, Linda realized she needed to accelerate her savings to retire comfortably. She worked with her financial advisor, Michael, to develop a retirement plan using the Sure Horizon Retirement Income Strategy™.

1. Essential Income

- **Maximized Catch-Up Contributions:** Increased her 401(k) contributions to the maximum allowable limit of $30,500 per year (including catch-up contributions). Michael's advice was to make these 401k contributions ROTH contributions to maximize tax efficiency after retirement.

- **Delay Retirement:** Linda postponed retirement to age 70, using those two extra years for additional savings.

- **Indexed Deferred Annuity:** Michael worked with Linda to take some of her funds and purchase an Indexed Deferred Annuity. This was funded with $60,000 of after-tax money from savings to generate efficient distributions when she reaches retirement. This annuity has a surrender charge, so Linda was less likely to raid this fund for non-essential expenses over the next 10 years. Since her income can vary in years that the real estate market is good, Linda used this as an additional retirement savings vehicle through her final 10 working years.

- **Social Security Planning:** Since she decided to delay retirement by 2 years, she also delayed Social Security benefits until age 70 to maximize monthly payouts. This will add about 15% more monthly to her retirement income from Social Security.

2. Discretionary Income

Linda realized that for her plan to work, she needed to reduce some expenses in her business and her personal life. However, she also liked to shop regularly. She knew if money was sitting around, it would get spent. Michael helped Linda create a sinking fund of about $40,000, using a bond ladder with the money.

- **Bond Ladder:** Set up a 5-year bond ladder that would begin to mature in a year. Instead of using this money during the first 10 years, when a bond matured, it would be reinvested in a new 5-year bond until Linda reached retirement. Michael purchased a mix of Treasury and investment-grade corporate bonds with staggered maturities. The ladder would provide about $12,000 annually starting at age 70 when she retires. All interest payments for the first 10 years were reinvested into the ladder.

3. Growth Pool

- **Asset Allocation Adjustments:** Shifted from a conservative portfolio to a more aggressive allocation to improve her returns and give her portfolio more growth:

  - Stocks: 70%

  - Bonds: 20%

  - REITs: 10%

- **Roth IRA Contributions:** She opened a Roth IRA and contributed $7,000 annually (including catch-up contributions).

- **Real Estate Investments:** She decided to purchase five rental properties over the next five years, each generating about $500 positive cash flow per month. Since she already manages properties for some existing clients, she will manage these properties and save herself the cost of a property manager. She used the excess cash flow to continue funding her retirement portfolio.

- **Consistent Rebalancing:** Working with Michael, Linda rebalanced her portfolio annually to maintain her new growth-focused allocation.

Outcome

By age 68, Linda will have significantly improved her retirement outlook, retiring with over $850,000 in her accounts and 7 Rental Properties with a Net Value after mortgages of $975,000. Here's how her retirement income breaks down:

1. Essential Income

- **Fixed Income Annuity (funded with a Tax-Free 1035 transfer from her Indexed Deferred Annuity):** Provides $2785 per month for life.

- **Social Security:** Monthly benefits of $2,600 starting at age 70.

- **Rental Property Income:** While not guaranteed, Linda's properties provide consistent monthly rental income. With consistent rent increases and strategic refinance, she can exceed inflation and increase her income over time. Linda's monthly cash flow is $5600 positive.

With all her guaranteed or low-risk income sources, Linda's total income covering Essential Income is slightly over $120,000 annually. The best part is that this income is highly tax efficient and does not result in taxation of her Social Security benefits.

2. Discretionary Income

At 70, Linda began to use her bond ladder to earn Discretionary Income. Here is what that looks like for her:

- **Bond Ladder:** Provides $12,000 per year for travel and leisure.

- **Dividend Portfolio:** Earns an additional $8,000 annually from high-yield dividend stocks that she began putting money into over the 10 years with Michael's help.

- **Work:** When she turned 68, Linda realized she wasn't ready to "Retire" yet and began working with people her age looking to downsize into smaller homes. She provides a concierge service that helps them prepare their existing home for sale, downsize their possessions, and then find a newer, smaller home. This new career has her working only about 15-20 hours per week when she wants to work and helps to provide an additional $40,000 - $50,000 per year. Most of Linda's clients now are old clients she has stayed in touch with over the years or made friends with. This has decreased her marketing expenses significantly.

3. Growth Pool

Linda's growth pool has grown to over $650,000 in investments and almost $975,000 in her Real Estate portfolio net worth.

- **Sustainable Withdrawals:** Michael encouraged Linda to set up her Discretionary Income Pool over 10 years ago so she did not have to pull that money out of her Growth Pool at retirement. That gave her an additional 5 years before she needed to fully refund that pool. Her required rate of return, in this case, is -1.92. Anything over that is a huge win for her and will increase her sustainability.

- **Rental Property Portfolio:** As discussed under Discretionary Income, the properties average around $5600 monthly positive cash flow. The other 3 benefits that Linda receives from her real estate investments are:

  - **Amortization:** Every month, as her renters pay her their rent, Linda pays her mortgage with the money, reducing her overall debt on the property.

  - **Depreciation:** One of the most significant benefits of real estate is the ability to depreciate the property over 27.5 years. That depreciation offsets the property's income, reducing Linda's income. Linda still pockets the $5600 per month, but depreciation reduces that by almost $35,000 annually.

  - **Appreciation:** While Linda's property is depreciating in the eyes of the IRS, it appreciates in value over time. In Linda's area, this has resulted in an average of about 6.5% over the time she has owned the properties.

Lessons Learned

Linda's story provides valuable lessons for late starters:

- **Maximize Catch-Up Contributions:** Use 401(k) and IRA catch-up contributions to rapidly boost retirement savings.

- **Utilize Immediate Annuities:** Immediate annuities provide guaranteed income and can secure essential expenses.

- **Diversify Income Sources:** Rental properties and dividend stocks offer additional discretionary income streams.

- **Don't Hang Up Your Spurs Too Soon:** Linda's decision to pivot her business to something that is a passion for her has allowed her to keep working without dreading getting up daily.

- **Delay Social Security Benefits:** Delaying Social Security to age 70 maximized her monthly payouts.

Key Takeaways

Linda's story shows you can secure a comfortable retirement with the right strategies, even starting late.

In the following case study, we'll meet John, an executive who used his high earnings to balance significant assets while planning for early retirement. Stay tuned!

Scenario 3: John adjusts to life's curveballs

Meet John, a retiree who faced an unexpected financial challenge just two years after retirement. As a former project manager, John prided himself on careful planning and attention to detail. At age 62, he retired comfortably with his wife, Mary. He looked forward to spending his golden years traveling and pursuing hobbies. That is what they did for the first two years following their plan. Two years after John retired, he was diagnosed with a health condition. Here are the details of John's situation:

- **Age:** 67, Mary 66

- **Profession:** Retired Project Manager/Mary Medical Office Manager

- **Retirement Savings:** $1.2 million

- **Essential Income:** $45,000 annually (Social Security and annuities)

- **Discretionary Income Fund:** $20,000 per year

- **Growth Pool Allocation:**

  - **Stocks:** 60%

  - **Bonds:** 30%

  - **REITs:** 10%

Challenges:

Two years into retirement, John was diagnosed with a heart condition that required costly surgery and long-term care for him to get back on his feet. To add to his challenges, John experienced a market downturn at the same time as his health issues.

- **Health Issues:** Diagnosed with a heart condition requiring costly surgery and long-term care. Initially, this caused severe issues with his mobility, requiring extra care.

- **Financial Setback:** The market downturn significantly impacted his Growth Pool.

Strategy Implemented

After receiving the diagnosis and learning about the market downturn, John and Mary realized they needed to adjust their financial plan immediately. To weather the storm, they used the Sure Horizon Retirement Income Strategy™.

1. Essential Income

- **Immediate Annuity:** John had previously purchased an immediate annuity that provided $2500 monthly for essential expenses. This stable piece of his portfolio gave them guarantees about the market uncertainty and John's health situation.

- **Social Security:** John had initially planned to postpone taking his social security payments until age 70 to take advantage of the increase. They made a decision to take Mary's at Full Retirement Age. Her payments are $1250 per month. As a result of the market downturn and John's health issue, and on the advice of their financial advisor, Ann, they decided to take John's social security at 68. This gave them an additional monthly Social Security benefit of $2,350, 7.6% more than if he had taken it at Full Retirement Age.

- **Long-Term Care Insurance:** John and Mary have a Long-Term Care policy that covers 75% of his long-term care costs, reducing the financial burden. This also allowed him and Mary to hire a home healthcare worker to come into their home each day and provide care Mary would have otherwise had to deliver.

2. Discretionary Income

- **Bond Ladder Adjustments:** Due to John's healthcare issue, they could not travel as much as they had planned. Working with Ann, they used the annual distributions from their bond ladder for the last three years to cover the additional costs of John's healthcare while still having money available to do some fun things to keep his spirits up.

- **Dividend Portfolio:** Ann also shifted some money from their growth portfolio into high dividend equities to provide more stability and additional income as needed, providing $5,000 annually.

3. Growth Pool

Asset Allocation Adjustments: Due to the uncertainty of John and Mary's situation, Ann also shifted to a more conservative allocation to reduce risk:

- **Stocks:** 45%

- **Bonds:** 40%

- **REITs:** 15%

This allocation adjustment provides more stability in the case of John's health not improving and the need to create additional guaranteed income by shifting funds to the Essential Income Pool.

- **Emergency Savings:** Ann also used part of his Growth Pool as an emergency savings fund, covering out-of-pocket medical expenses and unexpected costs in the early years of his condition.

- **Roth IRA Withdrawals:** To maximize John and Mary's Social Security Payments, they made tax-free withdrawals from his Roth IRA to cover the remaining 25% of long-term care costs. This allowed them to not be taxed on their Social Security benefits.

Outcome

Despite facing a significant health issue and financial setbacks, John and Mary managed to maintain their financial stability and lifestyle. Three years after his initial health scare, he and Mary could travel again and enjoy retirement. This allowed them to continue with their original plans and travel. As a result of the market downturn, John and Mary, with Ann's suggestion, decided to only refund their Discretionary Pool a year after it was exhausted (allowing another year for the market to recover). Since John had elected to take his Social Security earlier than planned, they could use that additional money instead of the discretionary funds for that year. After the market had recovered, they rebuilt their Discretionary Pool after what would have been year 6 of the original plan.

Lessons Learned

John's story offers valuable lessons for retirees:

- **Maintain Flexibility:** Be prepared to adjust discretionary spending and Growth Pool withdrawals in response to financial setbacks. Mike Tyson said, "Everyone has a plan until they get punched in the face."

- **Essential Income Security:** Annuities and Social Security provided a steady income stream for essential expenses. Those guaranteed payments helped during a time of health insecurity and mitigated the impact of the market downturn.

- **Emergency Savings Fund:** A dedicated emergency savings fund ensures immediate liquidity for unexpected costs. Ann shifted some growth portfolios to provide this additional liquidity as the situation happened.

- **Long-term care insurance** protects John from catastrophic medical expenses. It also provided home-based care, which allowed John to stay home to recover and allowed Mary to not have to provide care that she could not physically perform.

Key Takeaways

John's story is a testament to the importance of comprehensive and flexible retirement planning. One of the true benefits of using the 3 x 3 Retirement Income Plan is the ability to adapt to life's challenges.

Conclusion

The case studies presented in this chapter highlight the real-world application of the strategies outlined in the 3 x 3 Retirement Income Plan. Whether you're an early planner, a late starter, or someone facing unexpected challenges, there's always a path to a secure and fulfilling retirement.

Key Lessons Learned

1. Plan Proactively

Early planning offers the most flexibility, but even late starters can succeed with the right strategies. Paul and Linda leveraged catch-up contributions, immediate annuities, and diversified portfolios to build solid financial futures.

2. Maintain flexibility

Flexibility is crucial. As John's story illustrates, maintaining emergency savings and adjusting discretionary spending ensures you can weather unexpected financial setbacks.

3. Secure Your Essential Income

Guaranteed income sources like Social Security, pensions, and annuities provide a stable foundation to cover essential expenses and offer peace of mind.

4. Diversify Discretionary Income

Utilize bond ladders, dividend portfolios, and other alternative income streams to fund the enjoyable aspects of retirement. Part-time work, passive income, and home-based businesses can supplement if your portfolio does not support a complete Discretionary Income Pool.

5. Optimize the Growth Pool

A well-managed Growth Pool helps sustain discretionary spending and provides a safety net for unexpected expenses. Adjust your Growth Pool allocation based on your changing needs and market conditions.

Call to Action

Now that you've seen how others have navigated their retirement journeys, it's your turn to start planning. The next chapter will walk you through completing your 3 x 3 Retirement Income Strategy™ We will:

- **Review Your Plan:** Take stock of your current financial situation and outline your retirement goals.

- **Secure Your Income:** Ensure your essential expenses are covered by guaranteed income sources.

- **Build Your Bond Ladder:** Plan your discretionary income to fund your retirement dreams.

- **Manage Your Growth Pool:** Invest in a diversified Growth Pool to sustain your financial future.

Your retirement journey is unique, but with a clear plan and the right strategies, you can achieve the retirement lifestyle you've always envisioned.

We'll provide a comprehensive toolkit of practical tools, templates, worksheets, and checklists to help you build your Sure Horizon Retirement Income Strategy™.

Chapter 20

Bonus Chapter: Understanding Long Term Care Needs

"Retirement planning isn't a one-time task—it's a lifelong commitment to your future self."

Long-term care is more than just medical support—it's about maintaining your lifestyle when you're not as spry as you used to be. Whether you get help with daily activities at home or move to a facility providing extra care, it's all about living your best life at every stage.

Home care, adult day care, assisted living, and skilled nursing—these options are there to support you when the going gets tough. But here's the kicker: 70% of us will need long-term care after 65. Women often need care longer than men—about 3.7 years on average, compared to 2.2 years for men. And it's not cheap. Full-time home care can run around $50,000 a year, while a private room in a nursing home might cost you over $105,000 annually. These are numbers that can significantly impact any retirement plan.

Defining Long-Term Care

Long-term care is about more than just nursing homes and hospitals. It's a spectrum of services designed to help people with chronic illnesses or disabilities live as independently as possible. Here's a quick rundown of what it includes:

- **Home Care:** Assistance with daily activities like bathing, dressing, and meal preparation, provided in the comfort of your home.

- **Adult Day Care Services:** Supervised programs offering social activities, therapy, and care during daytime hours.

- **Assisted Living Facilities:** Housing options that offer personal care services, social activities, and medical support in a community setting.

- **Nursing Homes:** Facilities providing round-the-clock skilled nursing care for those with significant medical needs.

- **Memory Care Units:** Specialized care environments catering to individuals with dementia or Alzheimer's.

Risks to Retirement Planning

Imagine you're retired, enjoying life, and then boom—long-term care needs come knocking. Not only can this deplete your savings, but it also puts a strain on your loved ones, who might have to step in as caregivers. Emotional, physical, and financial strains are natural and often overlooked. Let's be honest—managing long-term care costs is like trying to tame a wild horse—challenging but not impossible with the right strategy.

Financial Impact

The cost of long-term care can chew through your retirement savings like termites on a wooden porch. Here's what it looks like in practical terms:

1. **Home Care Costs:** You might prefer to receive care at home, but the bills can pile up faster than expected. At $27 an hour for a home health aide, full-time care can set you back about $50,000 a year. Multiply that by a few years, and suddenly, your nest egg looks more like a chicken coop.

2. **Assisted Living Facilities:** Cost an average of $4,500, up to over $54,000 a year. And that's just for the basics—amenities like specialized memory care or private suites come with a hefty premium.

3. **Nursing Home Expenses:** If you need the round-the-clock care of a nursing home, brace yourself for a bigger hit. A private room averages $105,000 yearly, while a semi-private one costs around $90,000. In a few short years, your

hard-earned savings could be toast.

Impact on Spouses and Families

Even if you've got substantial retirement savings, long-term care expenses can quickly leave your spouse in a financial bind:

- **Reduced Income:** If your spouse needs to cut back on work to care for you, that's less money coming in.

- **Depleted Savings:** Drawing down your retirement savings for care can leave your spouse scrambling to cover their future needs.

- **Reverse Mortgages or Downsizing:** Some retirees consider a reverse mortgage or downsizing their home to cover care costs, but these decisions often come with emotional baggage.

Long-term care isn't just a financial challenge – it can turn your family's world upside down. For the direct family caregivers such as the spouse or adult children, this can lead to:

- **Emotional Stress:** Caring for a loved one can be emotionally draining, leading to feelings of guilt, anxiety, and helplessness.

- **Physical Fatigue:** The physical demands of caregiving, such as lifting and transferring, can leave caregivers exhausted and prone to injury.

- **Quality of Care Concerns:** When family members provide care, there's often a lack of professional training, which can affect the quality of care and lead to burnout.

- **Sibling Conflicts:** Disagreements about caregiving responsibilities or financial contributions can strain sibling relationships.

- **Marital Tension:** Caring for in-laws or managing caregiving alongside a spouse's career can strain marriages.

Ignoring the risks of long-term care can throw a wrench into your retirement plans, leaving you and your loved ones with financial headaches and emotional heartaches. The key is to have a proactive strategy in place, one that addresses both the economic and emotional challenges head-on.

In the next section, we'll tackle common misconceptions about long-term care and how to build a solid plan for these potential pitfalls.

Types of Insurance Available Help Pay For Care

Navigating the world of long-term care insurance can feel like exploring a vast menu of options, each with its benefits and drawbacks. Whether you're leaning towards a traditional plan or considering something more modern, understanding your choices is crucial.

Traditional Long-Term Care Insurance

This is the classic choice, explicitly designed to cover the broad spectrum of long-term care needs. Here's what makes these policies stand out:

- **Coverage**: They typically cover everything from home care and assisted living to adult day care and nursing home services.

- **Flexibility in Benefits**: You can choose from various benefit periods, like a couple of years to a lifetime, with daily benefit limits that you select based on your needs.

- **Inflation Protection**: To keep up with rising costs, you can add riders to incrementally increase your benefits over time.

- **Waiting Periods**: These policies usually have a deductible period, often 30 to 90 days, which works like a deductible before the benefits kick in.

The upside? They offer comprehensive coverage and options to protect against inflation. The downside? Premiums can increase over time, and if you never use the benefits, your premiums don't come back to you.

Hybrid Life Insurance with Long-Term Care Riders

If you're looking for a two-in-one solution, these hybrid policies might be up your alley. They combine life insurance with long-term care benefits:

- **Life Insurance Benefit**: If you don't use the long-term care portion, there's a death benefit for your beneficiaries.

- **Long-Term Care Benefit**: You can tap into the death benefit early to cover long-term care costs.

- **Return of Premium**: Some policies even allow you to get your premiums back if you decide the coverage no longer meets your needs.

They're great because they lock in your premiums and cover two significant needs with one policy. However, they tend to be pricier than traditional plans and might not cover a broader range of services.

Critical Illness Insurance

While not a direct substitute for long-term care insurance, critical illness coverage can complement your plan by providing a lump sum if you're diagnosed with a severe illness like cancer or Alzheimer's. Typically, there is a lump sum benefit that you receive as a one-time payment that can be used for various expenses, including some long-term care costs.

It's generally more affordable than traditional long-term care insurance. Still, it's limited to specific diagnoses, and the payout might only partially cover some of your long-term care needs.

Choosing the Right Policy

Think of picking a policy like choosing the perfect dessert to suit your taste and dietary needs! Here's what to consider:

- **Coverage Needs**: Make sure the policy covers the types of care you anticipate needing.

- **Cost Considerations**: Understand the premium structure—can you lock in rates, or might they increase over time?

- **Inflation Protection**: Consider options that increase your benefit amount annually to keep pace with cost increases.

- **Health and Age Factors**: Buying a policy when younger can reduce costs, but be aware of medical underwriting that could affect eligibility.

- **Insurer's Reputation**: Check ratings and reviews to gauge the insurer's financial stability and claim payment history.

Long-term care insurance isn't one-size-fits-all. By understanding the different types of policies and what each offers, you can better navigate this complex landscape and choose a plan that aligns with your health, lifestyle, and financial goals. As we move forward, we'll explore alternative ways to fund long-term care, providing you with a comprehensive view of your options.

Understanding What Qualifies For Long-Term Care Insurance

In addition to understanding the various insurance options available, it's crucial to grasp precisely what qualifies as long-term care. This term broadly refers to a range of services. Support is needed when a person is unable to perform activities of daily living (ADLs) due to chronic illness, disability, or aging.

Defining Activities of Daily Living (ADLs)

Activities of daily living include essential tasks that are fundamental to caring for oneself and maintaining independence. The six primary ADLs are:

- **Bathing**: The ability to clean oneself and perform grooming activities like shaving and brushing teeth.

- **Dressing**: The ability to make appropriate clothing decisions and physically dress oneself.

- **Eating**: The ability to feed oneself, though not necessarily the capability to prepare food.

- **Transferring**: The ability to move from one place to another while performing activities, such as getting out of bed or a chair.

- **Toileting**: The ability to get to and from the toilet, use it appropriately, and clean oneself.

- **Continence**: The ability to control bladder and bowel functions.

When an individual can no longer independently manage these activities, long-term care services become necessary to assist in daily living. Depending on the level of support needed, this care can be provided at home, in a community setting, or within a facility. For Long-Term Care Insurance to take effect, two or more of your ADLs must be affected.

The necessity for long-term care arises from the natural aging process and various health conditions that can impair physical and mental abilities. By incorporating long-term care planning into your retirement strategy, you ensure that these needs are met without compromising your financial stability or placing undue burden on your loved ones.

Alternatives to Long-Term Care Insurance

Self-Insurance

So, maybe you're not sold on long-term care insurance. Perhaps you're thinking, "I can handle this alone." That's what we call self-insurance.

Is Self-Insurance Right for You?

Self-insurance means you rely on your savings and investments to cover long-term care costs. It's not for everyone, but it might work if you have a healthy retirement fund and a solid income stream.

1. **Start by Estimating Costs:** Get a realistic idea of what care might cost you. Remember, we're talking about tens of thousands of dollars annually. Run the numbers and see if your portfolio can handle it.

2. **Earmark Funds for Care:** Set aside a chunk of your retirement savings for long-term care. Consider creating a separate investment account or setting up a "healthcare sinking fund."

3. **Balance Growth and Safety:** Invest those funds in a way that balances growth and safety. You want enough growth to keep up with inflation but not too much

risk that market swings could wipe out your savings.

4. **Include Your Family:** Make sure your spouse and family members know about your self-insurance strategy so they can plan accordingly.

Medicaid Strategies

Talking about Medicaid as a long-term care safety net can be daunting. Knowing all your options is essential, especially if the traditional insurance route is out of reach. Here's a more straightforward breakdown of how Medicaid might fit into your plan, especially if you're watching your budget closely.

Getting to Know Medicaid Eligibility

When planning for potential long-term care under Medicaid, it's critical to understand the "lookback" period. This rule can significantly impact eligibility. Medicaid scrutinizes asset transfers made within five years before applying for benefits. Suppose you transferred assets like a home or significant savings during this period. In that case, you might face penalties, such as a delay in receiving Medicaid benefits. This policy aims to prevent individuals from reducing their assets on paper to qualify for Medicaid. Therefore, it's essential for anyone considering Medicaid as part of their long-term care strategy to carefully plan asset transfers and consult with a financial advisor or elder law attorney to navigate these rules effectively.

Medicaid isn't just automatically available; it comes with its own set of rules, particularly around how much you can own and still qualify. There's a cap on what you can have in the bank — typically around $2,000 to $3,000, though it varies by state. If you're above this, you'll need to think about some legal ways to "spend down" your assets. If you're married and only one of you needs care, Medicaid tries to prevent your whole life savings from being swallowed up. They allow the healthier spouse to keep some assets and income, called the "Community Spouse Resource Allowance."

Strategies to Protect Your Assets

- **Spend Down Wisely**: You might consider spending down your assets on necessary healthcare expenses to fall within Medicaid's limits.

- **Annuities**: Specific types of annuities are designed to help meet Medicaid's rules by turning assets into income for the spouse who isn't in care.

- **Trusts**: Another strategy involves placing some assets in an irrevocable trust. However, keep in mind Medicaid's five-year lookback period. Any assets moved out of your control within five years before applying for Medicaid could penalize you.

Planning for the Future

Here's the kicker — after the Medicaid recipient passes away, the state might try to recoup what it spent on your care from your estate. Yes, that can include your home except in Homestead states. You might consider legally transferring your home to your spouse or children ahead of time. Or you might set up a life estate, which keeps the home out of the estate recovery process while allowing you to live there until you pass. Navigating Medicaid isn't simple and is not a one-size-fits-all solution. Still, careful planning and professional guidance can be crucial in managing your long-term care needs without depleting every penny of your savings.

Family and Community Support

Navigating the maze of long-term care isn't just a solo journey—your family and the wider community can be vital sources of support.

Family Caregiving: A Mixed Blessing

When it comes to long-term care, family members often step into the role of caregivers. This solution comes with its own set of challenges that we previously covered:

- **Financial Impact**: Caregiving can force some family members to reduce work hours or even quit their jobs, leading to financial strain.

- **Emotional Weight**: Caring for others can also be emotionally draining, sometimes causing burnout and strained family relationships.

Supporting Your Family CaregiversIt's crucial to ensure that those who care for you also receive support:

- **Respite Care**: Implementing respite care is essential. This could involve arranging temporary help from adult daycare services or home care assistance to give regular caregivers a much-needed break.

- **Community and Support Groups**: Encourage caregivers to connect with support groups where they can find solace and advice from others facing similar challenges.

Community Resources: A Broader Support Network Your local community can be an invaluable ally:

- **Senior Centers**: These hubs offer various programs, classes, and activities that provide support and socialization opportunities.

- **Volunteer Networks**: Groups like Meals on Wheels or local faith-based organizations often provide volunteer support for routine errands, companionship, and more.

- **Innovative Living Arrangements**: Explore emerging models like senior co-housing, which allows seniors to live together and support one another, or "Villages," community networks that enable members to assist each other in aging comfortably at home.

By tapping into these family and community resources, you can create a more sustainable and enriching care environment for yourself and your caregivers.

Long-term care planning doesn't have to rely solely on insurance policies. Whether self-insuring, exploring Medicaid options, or tapping into family and community support, the key is to have a proactive plan that aligns with your values and resources.

The following section will cover how Long-Term Care planning should be integrated into a Holistic Financial Plan.

Holistic Planning

Regarding retirement planning, think of long-term care as one piece of a much bigger puzzle. Your strategy should manage long-term care risks while allowing you to achieve your other retirement goals, like traveling, enjoying hobbies, or leaving a legacy.

Balancing Long-Term Care with Other Retirement Goals

1. **Secure Your Essential Income First:** Make sure your essential living expenses are covered with guaranteed income streams like Social Security, pensions, or annuities before you start thinking about long-term care.

2. **Build Your Discretionary Income Fund:** Create a 5-year fund for non-essential activities like travel and hobbies, separate from your long-term care funds.

3. **Allocate Funds for Long-Term Care:** Set aside specific funds for long-term care, whether through self-insurance, long-term care insurance, or Medicaid planning. This will protect your essential and discretionary income pools from being depleted.

4. **Include Family in Your Plans:** Have open conversations with your spouse and family members about your long-term care strategy. Discuss their potential roles and preferences in caregiving or managing finances.

5. **Estate Planning and Legacy Goals:** Ensure your estate plan reflects your long-term care strategy, especially if Medicaid planning or trusts are involved. Ensure your will, power of attorney, and healthcare directives are up-to-date.

Example Strategy: The 3 x 3 Retirement Income Plan with Long-Term Care

- **Essential Income:** Social Security, Pensions, Annuities

- **Discretionary Income:** Bond Ladder, Dividends

- **Growth Pool:** Equities, Mutual Funds, ETFs

- **Long-Term Care Fund:** Dedicated savings, Long-term care insurance, Hybrid Life Insurance Plan, Critical Care Plan.

Regular Review and Adjustment

A solid plan today will only sometimes stay that way tomorrow. Life throws us curveballs, so it's essential to regularly review and adjust your long-term care strategy.

Conducting Regular Reviews

1. **Annual Health Review:** Check in with your doctor about any changes in your health or potential risk factors. This can guide adjustments to your long-term care strategy.

2. **Family Dynamics Assessment:** Have any changes occurred in your family that might affect your plan? For example:

   - A spouse or family member needs to take care of themselves.

   - Adult children are moving away or closer.

   - New grandchildren add joy (and potential financial considerations).

3. **Financial Resources Review:** Review your financial situation to ensure your long-term care funding remains on track.

   - If needed, adjust the allocation between your essential, discretionary, growth, and long-term care pools.

4. **Update Insurance Policies and Estate Plans:** Reassess your insurance policies for any gaps or changes needed. Update your will, power of attorney, and healthcare directives.

5. **Increasing Coverage or Funds:** If your health risk factors increase, consider increasing long-term care insurance coverage or adding more to your self-insurance fund.

6. **Reducing Coverage:** If you have a solid self-insurance fund, you may reduce

or drop specific insurance policies.

7. **Adjusting Medicaid Planning:** Revisit Medicaid eligibility and estate implications. If Medicaid seems more likely, consider transferring assets to an irrevocable trust.

Integrating long-term care into your retirement plan requires a holistic approach. You must balance your other goals while staying adaptable to life's changes.

Effective long-term care planning shouldn't be siloed from your other retirement planning efforts; it should be a seamless part of your overall strategy. This means regularly revisiting your plan to adjust for changes in your health, family dynamics, or financial situation. It's about staying flexible and responsive to life's unpredictable nature.

In the next section, we will look at case studies of individuals and families who are facing long-term care challenges.

Case Study: Jim and Carol, the "Prepared Couple"

Their Story

Jim and Carol, a couple in their mid-60s, are the very picture of preparedness. They seem to have it all figured out with two children, healthy retirement savings, and a comfortable lifestyle. However, beneath the surface, there are worries. Jim's family has a history of Alzheimer's, and Carol fears the financial strain of unexpected healthcare costs.

Facing the Challenge

Determined not to let these fears overshadow their golden years, Jim and Carol took proactive steps. Jim, aware of his heightened risk of Alzheimer's due to his family history, and Carol, concerned about maintaining their lifestyle, decided on a dual strategy.

Strategic Planning

- **Jim's Self-Insurance Plan**: Due to Jim's family history and the beginnings of some memory issues, Jim had difficulty finding a Long Term Care Policy that they could afford. Ultimately, they earmarked $300,000 for Jim's potential long-term care needs. This fund was calculated to cover the average costs of Alzheimer's care, considering Jim's personal risk factors.

- **Carol's Insurance Safeguard**: Carol opted for a traditional long-term care insurance policy. She chose a policy with a 3-year benefit period and a daily benefit of $200, ensuring her care needs would be met without jeopardizing their financial stability.

Estate and Legal Preparations

Understanding the importance of legal preparedness, they updated their wills and health-care directives to clearly reflect their current wishes. They also established durable powers of attorney for each other and their eldest daughter, ensuring that decision-making could continue smoothly should one become incapacitated.

A Secure Outcome

Today, Jim and Carol enjoy peace of mind, knowing they are well-prepared. Their strategy ensures that if Jim ever requires long-term care, they won't need to dip into their primary savings, thus protecting Carol's financial future. Meanwhile, Carol's insurance provides a safety net for her own care needs.

Key Takeaways

Jim and Carol's story underscores the importance of tailored planning. Combining self-insurance with a targeted insurance policy, they've crafted a personalized strategy addressing each concern. Moreover, their open communication with their children about these plans ensures that the whole family is prepared for whatever may come, reinforcing the idea that early and informed planning is crucial in navigating the uncertainties of aging.

Case Study 2: Susan's Strategic Medicaid Planning

Meet Susan

At 72, Susan is a widow without children, living modestly from a $1,500 monthly Social Security check. Her main asset is her home, valued at $250,000. Life threw a curveball when she was diagnosed with early-stage Parkinson's disease, sparking concerns about her future care needs and the financial burden they could bring.

Facing Reality

With limited savings and the looming costs of potential long-term care, Susan faced a financial puzzle. How could she ensure quality care without risking losing her home or depleting her meager funds?

Strategic Moves for Medicaid Eligibility

Susan decided to delve into Medicaid planning with the help of an elder law attorney. Here's what they did:

- **Setting Up an Irrevocable Trust**: Susan placed her home and savings into an irrevocable trust, safeguarding her assets from being counted towards Medicaid's stringent asset limits.

- **Navigating the Lookback Period**: By transferring her assets five years before applying for Medicaid, Susan started the clock on the mandatory lookback period, a critical step to avoid penalties and ensure eligibility.

Building a Support System

Without children, Susan turned to her nieces and nephews, who assisted with caregiving decisions and managed the trust.

A Secure Outcome

Five years after setting up the trust, Susan's planning paid off. She qualified for Medicaid and moved into a comfortable nursing home, confident that her house was secure. The trust she established now generated rental income, supplementing her Social Security and providing extra funds for her personal needs.

Reflections on the Journey

Susan's journey into Medicaid planning highlights the importance of early and strategic action. By understanding the rules and planning accordingly, she protected her assets and secured the care she needed. Her story is a powerful lesson on the effectiveness of early planning, particularly the critical role of the five-year lookback period and the benefits of establishing an irrevocable trust to ensure ongoing care without sacrificing financial security.

Case Study 3: Alex and Maria's Sandwich Generation Strategy

Meet Alex and Maria

At 55, Alex and Maria find themselves in a typical sandwich generation dilemma. They're juggling the financial demands of their two college-aged children and the daily care needs of Alex's 80-year-old mother, who lives with them. Maria has taken on the role of primary caregiver, a commitment that's as rewarding as it is challenging.

Confronting Their Reality

With their family's complex dynamics, Alex and Maria needed a plan to secure their financial future while managing the immediate care needs of Alex's mother. They also needed to balance the hefty expenses of college tuition with their own retirement and long-term care planning.

A Strategic Approach to Care and Finances

- **Hybrid Life Insurance with Long-Term Care Rider**: They chose a hybrid policy offering a dual benefit—a $500,000 death benefit and up to $200 per day for long-term care for five years. This versatile policy provided peace of mind, knowing they could access long-term care benefits if needed without compromising the death benefit for their children.

- **Leveraging Community Support**: They tapped into local resources to lessen Maria's caregiving load, engaging with senior centers and adult daycare programs that offered Alex's mother daytime activities and social interactions.

- **Creating a Financial Cushion**: Understanding the importance of self-care and maintaining their lifestyle, Alex and Maria established a discretionary income fund. They used a bond ladder strategy to ensure this fund would support activities like travel and dining out, which provided necessary breaks and stress relief.

A Future-Proofed Outcome

Today, Alex and Maria are more confident about handling whatever comes their way. They've alleviated some caregiving burdens and secured a plan supporting their immediate and future financial needs. Their children fully know the family's strategies, ensuring open communication and understanding about future economic and care responsibilities.

Valuable Takeaways

Alex and Maria's journey underscores the effectiveness of hybrid insurance policies as a flexible tool for managing death benefits and long-term care expenses. Their experience also highlights the critical role of community resources in supporting caregiving families, helping to prevent caregiver burnout, and improving the quality of life for all family members. Their proactive measures in planning and communication are lessons in balancing the demands of the sandwich generation with grace and foresight.

Case Study 4: Mark's Crisis Navigation

Introducing Mark

Mark, at 67, found himself facing an unexpected challenge after retiring. Living alone and recently diagnosed with early-stage dementia, he confronted the harsh reality that his savings were inadequate for the long-term care he suddenly needed. With no family nearby to lean on, Mark had to quickly figure out a sustainable care solution.

Navigating Through Crisis

- **Critical Illness Insurance Comes Through:** Fortunately, Mark had taken out a critical illness insurance policy that provided a lump sum payout of $100,000 upon his diagnosis. This financial relief came at a crucial time, giving him the means to address his immediate care needs.

- **Securing Steady Income with an Immediate Annuity**: Mark invested his insurance payout into an immediate annuity to ensure a continuous income stream. This intelligent move now supplies him with $1,000 each month for life, offering stability in his financial planning.

- **Utilizing Medicaid for Home-Based Care**: Mark took advantage of a community-based Medicaid program, which enabled him to receive essential home care services. This allowed him to manage his daily activities with professional help and stay in the comfort of his own home.

A Managed Outcome

Thanks to his critical illness payout and the strategic use of an immediate annuity, Mark has managed to secure the necessary care without exhausting his savings. His enrollment in Medicaid's community-based care program supports his desire to maintain some degree of independence despite his medical condition.

Reflecting on the Lessons

Mark's situation highlights the crucial role of critical illness insurance when unexpected health issues arise, especially when other long-term care arrangements are not in place. It also demonstrates the value of Medicaid's community programs in providing practical, in-home support that can dramatically improve the quality of life for those with chronic health issues. This case is a powerful reminder of the importance of planning for health contingencies and leveraging available insurance and support systems to navigate life's unexpected challenges.

These case studies show how different strategies can be tailored to your needs and circumstances. By learning from these examples, you can create a proactive long-term care plan that aligns with your financial goals.

In the next section, we'll dive into exercises and worksheets to help you develop your strategy.

Estimating Your Long-Term Care Costs

A long-term care cost calculator helps you estimate potential expenses based on location, type of care, and expected duration. It's essential for anyone planning to self-insure or aiming to determine the right level of insurance coverage. In this exercise, we will use two different calculators (one from AARP and the other from our friends at Dinkytown).

1. **Estimating Costs Per Month:** The first number you need to understand is the cost of care in your area. The easiest way to assess this is by using the Long Term Care Cost Calculator on AARP's website *(https://www.aarp.org/caregiving/fin*

ancial-legal/long-term-care-cost-calculator.html). You put your zip code in at the top, and the calculator will give you the following:

- **Cost of Non-Residential Care** (Home Health Care Aids)

- **Assisted Living Cost**

- **Semi-Private Nursing Home**

- **Private Nursing Home**

2. **The Cost to Self-Insure:** Now, you must know what you need to save to self-insure. We will use the Long Term Care Calculator from my favorite calculator website, Dinkytown.com (https://www.dinkytown.net/java/long-term-care-calculator.html#), which will give you the estimated cost of what you would need to have saved today to cover long-term care costs.

Introduction to Comparing Long-Term Care Insurance Policies

Navigating the complex landscape of long-term care insurance can be challenging. Still, planning for your future health and financial well-being is crucial. This exercise, involving the completion of the Insurance Policy Comparison Worksheet, is designed to empower you by giving you the tools to compare different policies side-by-side. This systematic approach helps illuminate the varying coverage options, costs, and benefits, allowing you to make an informed decision that aligns with your personal and financial circumstances.

However, while this worksheet provides a robust framework for understanding and comparing insurance policies, the nuances of long-term care insurance can benefit significantly from professional guidance. Please take the initiative to contact a Long-Term Care Specialist in your area. These professionals specialize in this type of insurance and can provide personalized advice that considers your specific needs and goals.

Here's How to Get Started:

1. **Research Specialists**: Search engines like Google can be used to find long-term care insurance specialists. Look for professionals with strong reviews and ratings, and check their credentials to ensure they are qualified to offer advice on such

an important decision.

2. **Prepare Your Information**: Gather relevant financial documents before your appointment and consider your long-term healthcare desires and needs. This preparation will make your consultation more efficient and productive.

3. **Set Up an Appointment**: Contact the specialists you've identified and schedule a consultation. Many specialists offer an initial consultation free of charge, which can be a valuable opportunity to assess their expertise and compatibility with your needs.

4. **Use the Worksheet**: Bring the Insurance Policy Comparison Worksheet you completed to your appointment. This will help guide your discussion, ensuring that all critical aspects of each policy are covered and that you understand how each option fits into your financial landscape.

Why This Matters:

Long-term care insurance is more than just a policy; it's a critical component of your financial security as you age. The right policy can protect your savings, provide peace of mind, and ensure you receive the necessary care. Consulting with a specialist can enhance your understanding of the options and legalities and assist you in navigating the fine print that could significantly impact your future.

By completing this worksheet and consulting with a specialist, you are taking proactive steps toward securing your future. This exercise equips you with the necessary information. It prepares you to engage in a meaningful dialogue with a professional who can tailor their advice to your situation.

Embrace this opportunity to invest in your future. The decisions you make today about long-term care insurance can ensure that your healthcare needs are met with dignity and that your finances are preserved.

Long Term Care Insurance Comparison Worksheet			
	Policy Name / Company	Policy Name / Company	Policy Name Company
Features			
Type of Policy (Traditional/Hybrid)			
Type of Care Covered			
Max Daily Benefit			
Benefit Period			
Premium			
Deductible			
Out of Pocket Maximum			
Inflation Protection			
Waiver of Premium			
Restoration of Benefits			
Exclusions and Limitations			
Additional Benefits			
Financial Ratings and Reviews			

Figure 20.1: Long Term Care Comparison Worksheet

Instructions for Completing the Insurance Policy Comparison Worksheet

Introduction:

This worksheet is designed to help you compare different long-term care insurance policies side-by-side. By filling out this worksheet, you can easily visualize the differences in coverage, costs, exclusions, and benefits among various policies. Follow the steps below to complete the table accurately.

Step 1: Gather Policy Information

Before you begin, collect all relevant documentation for each insurance policy you wish to compare. This might include brochures, product disclosure statements, or quotes provided by insurance companies.

Step 2: Label Each Column

- Assign each policy a column in the worksheet. The first column on the left is reserved for the features and terms you will compare.

- At the top of each subsequent column, write the name of the insurance policy and the company offering it (e.g., Policy A - Company X, Policy B - Company Y).

Step 3: Fill in the Details for Each Policy

- **Type of Care Covered**: Note what each policy covers, such as in-home care, nursing home care, or assisted living facilities.

- **Maximum Daily/Monthly Benefit**: Enter the maximum amount that the policy will pay per day or month.

- **Benefit Period**: Specify the duration for which benefits are payable under each policy (e.g., 3 years, 5 years, lifetime).

- **Premium**: List the cost of each policy, noting whether these are paid monthly, annually, etc.

- **Deductible**: If applicable, include the deductible amount that must be paid out-of-pocket before the insurance begins to pay.

- **Out-of-Pocket Maximum**: Note the maximum out-of-pocket expenses the insured must pay annually.

- **Inflation Protection**: Indicate whether each policy includes inflation protection, and if so, what type (e.g., none, simple, compound).

- **Waiver of Premium**: Describe the conditions under which premiums are waived (e.g., once you start receiving benefits).

- **Restoration of Benefits**: Explain if and how benefits can be restored after use.

- **Exclusions and Limitations**: List any specific exclusions or limitations each policy has, such as exclusions for pre-existing conditions or particular diseases.

- **Additional Benefits**: Include any extra features like respite care or international coverage.

- **Financial Ratings and Reviews**: Provide the financial strength ratings from recognized agencies and summarize any notable customer reviews or satisfaction ratings.

Step 4: Review and Compare

Once all the information has been entered, review the completed worksheet to compare the policies. Look for:

- The most comprehensive coverage.

- The most affordable premiums concerning the benefits offered.

- Any significant exclusions or limitations that could affect your decision.

Step 5: Decision Making

Use the completed table to identify the policy that best meets your needs based on coverage, costs, and benefits. When making your decision, consider your health, financial situation, and long-term care needs.

Additional Tips:

- Always verify the information with an insurance agent or provider to ensure accuracy.

- Consult a financial advisor or insurance broker to discuss your needs and circumstances.

By methodically filling out the insurance policy comparison worksheet, you will be better equipped to decide which long-term care insurance policy best suits your requirements. This worksheet is valuable for simplifying complex information and highlighting the differences between various policies.

Conclusion: Navigating the Path to Long-Term Care

As we conclude this chapter on long-term care, it's essential to recognize that planning for future care is not just a financial exercise but a profound step towards ensuring dignity, comfort, and security in our later years. The journey through understanding and choosing long-term care options can seem daunting. Still, it is a necessary part of preparing for the uncertainties of aging.

Throughout this chapter, we've explored the various types of long-term care, the associated costs, and the importance of early planning. By comparing different insurance policies using the Insurance Policy Comparison Worksheet, you can make informed decisions that align with your needs and financial situation. We discussed the value of consulting with Long-Term Care Specialists to tailor a plan that fits your unique life circumstances.

Remember, your choices today about long-term care planning will have a lasting impact on your life and those of your loved ones. It's about more than just insurance; it's about crafting a strategy that supports your vision for the future. Consider the financial, emotional, and practical implications of your care choices. How you plan now can affect your quality of life and independence in the future.

As you move forward, keep revisiting your plan. Life changes, and so might your long-term care needs. Regular reviews with professionals can help you adjust your strategy to new life stages, health changes, or financial situations.

Let this chapter serve as a foundation for building a thoughtful, comprehensive approach to your long-term care. Take proactive steps, seek advice when needed, and choose options that provide peace of mind, knowing you are well-prepared for the future. In doing so, you are not just planning for care; you are planning for life.

Chapter 21

Bonus Chapter: Understanding Reverse Mortgages

"Retirement isn't an end—it's a new beginning. Make sure you're prepared to enjoy it."

Introduction: Navigating the World of Reverse Mortgages

As you approach the golden years of retirement, the financial planning landscape undergoes a significant shift. The decisions you make now, in the calm before the storm of retirement, can shape the quality and comfort of your later years. Among these decisions is the potential use of a reverse mortgage, a financial tool that, when understood and used strategically, can be a game-changer for those looking to optimize their financial resources during retirement.

For many of us, our home equity is a significant asset. The typical financial planning strategy is to have a fully paid-off home at retirement, do nothing with it, and then pass it on to your family after you and your spouse are no longer around. But let's face it, your family probably doesn't want your old house filled with your stuff, and they certainly don't want to fight over it.

In the Financial Media, financial gurus will tell you that Reverse Mortgages are "Horrible" and the "Worst thing that has ever occurred."" Similar to other financial vehicles we have discussed in this book, a Reverse Mortgage, when used with proper strategy, can further reduce investment risk in retirement.

Reverse mortgages allow homeowners aged 62 and older to convert part of the equity in their home into cash without having to sell their home or pay additional monthly bills. This might sound straightforward, but the intricacies warrant a more profound understanding to harness its benefits while avoiding common pitfalls.

Here's what we'll cover in this chapter:

- **Eligibility and Requirements:** Who qualifies, and what are the necessary conditions?

- **Strategic Uses in Retirement Planning:** How can a reverse mortgage fit your retirement strategy?

- **Advantages and Drawbacks:** What are the potential benefits, and what should you watch out for?

- **Choosing a Reputable Lender and Understanding the Impact on Estate Planning:** This will ensure that you make the right choices for the long term.

As we delve into the details, remember: the goal here isn't just to inform you but to equip you with the knowledge to make decisions that align with your retirement dreams and circumstances. Let's begin by understanding the basics of reverse mortgages and who qualifies for them.

Eligibility and Requirements for Reverse Mortgages

Before diving into the mechanics of reverse mortgages, it's crucial to understand who qualifies for this financial tool and what commitments it entails. Here's a straightforward breakdown:

Eligibility Criteria:

- **Age Requirement:** The primary borrower must be at least 62 years old. This age requirement ensures that the product is used as a retirement planning tool, helping those in their later years leverage their most significant asset—their home. In some states, such as my home state of Texas, all borrowers must be over 62.

- **Primary Residence:** The property in question must be your primary residence. This means that you live there for the majority of the year. Vacation homes or investment properties do not qualify.

- **Home Equity:** You should own your home outright or have a substantial amount of equity built up. Generally, it would help if you had at least 50% equity, which means your mortgage balance should be less than half the value of your home.

Property Requirements:

- The home must meet specific standards and be in good repair. Eligible properties include:

  - Single-family homes.

  - Multi-unit properties (up to four units), provided the borrower occupies one unit.

  - HUD-approved condominiums.

  - Manufactured homes that meet FHA requirements.

Homeowner Responsibilities:

While a reverse mortgage eliminates monthly mortgage payments, it does not absolve you of other financial responsibilities. You must continue paying property taxes, homeowner's insurance, and homeowners association (HOA) fees. Understanding and preparing for these obligations is a key part of responsible financial planning in retirement. Maintaining the condition of your home is not just about pride of ownership; it's a requirement. The home must be repaired to comply with the loan terms.

HUD Counseling Requirement:

A unique aspect of applying for a reverse mortgage is the requirement to consult with a HUD-approved counselor. This session ensures you understand all aspects of the loan, including its implications for your finances and estate planning.

Understanding these requirements is the first step toward determining if a reverse mortgage could be a viable part of your financial strategy in retirement. It's about making an informed decision considering your long-term needs and the legacy you wish to leave.

Strategic Uses of Reverse Mortgages in Retirement Planning

Reverse mortgages are about accessing cash and strategic financial management during retirement. Whether it's supplementing income, managing debts, or providing a safety net, this financial tool offers a variety of uses that can be tailored to individual retirement plans. Let's explore how they can be pivotal components of your financial strategy, putting you in the driver's seat of your retirement planning.

Supplementing Retirement Income

One of the primary benefits of a reverse mortgage is the ability to convert home equity into a steady income stream. This can be particularly valuable if other retirement funds are lower than expected or unexpected expenses arise.

Consider Mary, who finds her pension and Social Security benefits insufficient to cover her living expenses and medical bills. Mary can access additional monthly funds by opting for a reverse mortgage, alleviating financial stress without impacting her other retirement savings.

Managing Existing Debt:

Many retirees find themselves still carrying mortgage debt into their retirement years. A reverse mortgage can pay off these existing mortgages or other obligations, freeing up monthly income previously devoted to debt payments.

For example, John and Linda, a couple in their early 70s, use a reverse mortgage to clear their remaining $100,000 mortgage debt. This move eliminates their monthly payment of $800, significantly reducing their financial outgoings and enhancing their cash flow.

Liquidity and Financial Flexibility (The Lifeboat Strategy):

The reverse mortgage line of credit is a flexible tool that retirees can tap into as needed. This feature is invaluable during market downturns or unexpected expenditures, providing financial breathing room without liquidating investments at a loss.

For example, Sarah, who prudently set up a reverse mortgage line of credit, faces high medical bills due to an unexpected illness. Instead of dipping into her investment portfolio during a market low, she accesses her reverse mortgage funds, allowing her investment time to recover.

These strategic uses highlight the versatility of reverse mortgages, not just as a means of emergency funding but as integral components of a comprehensive retirement strategy. By understanding and leveraging these options, retirees can maintain a more comfortable and secure financial standing.

Advantages and Drawbacks of Reverse Mortgages

Reverse mortgages offer unique benefits that can enhance the financial flexibility of retirees. Still, they also come with certain drawbacks that need careful consideration. Understanding both sides of this financial tool will help you make an informed decision that aligns with your retirement goals and personal circumstances.

Advantages of Reverse Mortgages:

1. **Increased Financial Flexibility:** Unlike traditional loans, reverse mortgages do not require monthly repayments. This can significantly alleviate cash flow pressures, allowing retirees to use their limited income for other essential expenses. For example, George and Helen, both in their late 70s, eliminate their monthly mortgage payment of $1500 by taking out a reverse mortgage, improving their overall cash flow and reducing financial stress.

2. **Stay in Your Home While Accessing Equity:** With a reverse mortgage, you can access your home and the equity you've built. This is particularly important for many retirees who prefer the comfort and familiarity of their home over moving to a new location. Frank, at 73, uses a reverse mortgage to supplement his income, which allows him to maintain his standard of living without having to sell his beloved family home.

3. **Versatile Payout Options:** Whether you need a lump sum, a line of credit, regular monthly payments, or the elimination of mortgage payments, reverse mortgages can be customized to meet diverse financial needs and planning goals.

Drawbacks of Reverse Mortgages:

1. **Reduction in Home Equity:** The equity in your home decreases as you receive payments from a reverse mortgage, which could leave less for your heirs. This reduction can affect the inheritance you plan to leave behind. For example, Lisa took out a reverse mortgage, and over time, the accruing interest and fees significantly reduced the home's equity, complicating her plans to leave a substantial inheritance to her children.

2. **Costs and Fees:** Reverse mortgages often come with upfront costs, including origination fees, which can erode the money you actually get to use. The one good thing about these programs is that they are overseen federally, so these costs are standardized nationwide.

3. **Complex Implications for Heirs:** If your heirs wish to keep the home after you leave or move out permanently, they must repay the reverse mortgage balance, typically done by refinancing the home with a regular forward mortgage. The family has 9 months from the time of death to do this. If it does not make sense for the family to hold it, they can either sell it and pay off the bank or let it sell it. The bank would return that to the family if equity remains in the property after the sale. Suppose there is no equity, and the property is underwater (more money owed than equity). In that case, the heirs are not responsible for paying the overage.

Understanding these pros and cons is crucial for anyone considering a reverse mortgage as part of their retirement strategy. By weighing these factors, you can better determine if this financial tool aligns with your overall financial planning and legacy goals.

Choosing a Reputable Lender and Understanding the Impact on Estate Planning

When delving into reverse mortgages, the importance of selecting the right lender cannot be overstated. Simultaneously, understanding how a reverse mortgage will impact your estate planning is critical to preserving your legacy and intentions.

Choosing a Reputable Lender:

Choosing the right lender is much like choosing a partner for a long-term journey—it requires careful consideration and due diligence. Begin by exploring a variety of lenders. Just as you wouldn't buy the first car you test drive, you shouldn't accept the first reverse mortgage offer you receive. Compare their terms, review their fees, and evaluate their customer service records. A reputable lender will always be transparent about their fees and rates, providing a clear breakdown of all costs associated with the reverse mortgage. They should make you feel comfortable, answering all your questions without pressuring you to sign on the dotted line.

Additionally, meeting with a HUD-approved counselor is not just a formality; it's an essential and required step in the process. These counselors independently assess the reverse mortgage terms, ensuring you understand every detail before proceeding.

Impact on Estate Planning:

Discussing how a reverse mortgage affects your estate is as crucial as any other financial planning discussion. A reverse mortgage reduces the equity in your home, which might alter the amount you can leave to your heirs. If your home is your largest asset, tapping into a significant portion of its equity might leave less for your family than you intended. However, it's important to note that reverse mortgages are non-recourse loans. This means if the loan amount exceeds the value of your home when it comes time to pay it back, your heirs won't have to foot the bill for the difference.

This is why open communication with your family is vital. They must understand how a reverse mortgage affects their inheritance and the estate. Planning these conversations helps manage expectations and leads to more robust, comprehensive estate planning. It is beneficial to work with an estate planning attorney who can align your reverse mortgage with other aspects of your estate plan, like wills or trusts, ensuring your financial actions accurately reflect your long-term intentions.

Choosing the right lender and understanding the impact on your estate requires thoughtful consideration. Still, when done correctly, a reverse mortgage can be a practical component of your financial strategy, offering both immediate benefits and long-term peace of mind.

Conclusion: Is a Reverse Mortgage Right for You?

Deciding whether a reverse mortgage is right can feel like navigating a maze with many turns and potential pitfalls. However, when approached with the correct information and a clear understanding of your financial and personal circumstances, it can be vital in achieving a secure and comfortable retirement.

Here's what you should consider to determine if a reverse mortgage suits your needs:

Evaluating Your Financial Situation:

- Do you have significant equity in your home? A reverse mortgage is most beneficial for those with considerable equity.

- Are your current retirement savings and income streams sufficient to cover your daily living expenses and any unexpected costs that might arise?

- Are you carrying burdensome mortgage payments or other debts into retirement that a reverse mortgage could alleviate?

Understanding Your Retirement Goals:

- Is staying in your current home a priority for you as you age? A reverse mortgage allows you to remain in your home while accessing the equity you've built up.

- Are you looking for additional sources of income to supplement Social Security, pensions, or other retirement funds?

- How important is it for you to maintain financial flexibility through a line of credit or other payout options provided by a reverse mortgage?

Considering the Impact on Heirs and Your Estate:

- Are you comfortable that your heirs may inherit less home equity due to the reverse mortgage?

- Have you discussed the implications of a reverse mortgage with your family to ensure a clear understanding of the future?

Planning for the Long Term:

- Can you continue to meet the ongoing obligations of property taxes and homeowner's insurance and maintain your home in good condition?

- Have you consulted with a HUD-approved counselor to fully understand the long-term implications and terms of the reverse mortgage?

- Do you have a plan to manage long-term care costs or other significant expenses that might arise during retirement?

A reverse mortgage is not a one-size-fits-all solution. Still, for many, it provides a practical and effective means to enhance their financial security in retirement. By carefully weighing these considerations and discussing your options with financial advisors and family members, you can decide to meet your immediate financial needs and support your long-term retirement goals.

Chapter 22

Putting It All Together: Your Own 3 x 3 Retirement Income Plan

"The Retirement Income Equation isn't just about numbers—it's about creating a life you love."

Alright, my dear reader. We have had a long journey together. I'm thrilled to guide you through one of the most crucial projects you'll embark on—designing your Sure Horizon Retirement Income Strategy™. This plan, which we'll delve into in detail, is a comprehensive strategy that breaks down the complex world of retirement planning into three manageable parts: ensuring guaranteed income for essentials, flexible income for the joys of life, and growth income to secure your future. If you've ever felt overwhelmed by the sheer amount of advice or worried about your financial future as retirement approaches, this plan is your roadmap to clarity and confidence.

Why is this plan so vital? Simply put, it breaks down the complex world of retirement planning into three manageable parts: ensuring guaranteed income for essentials, flexible income for the joys of life, and growth income to secure your future. It's like constructing a house, where every piece needs to fit perfectly for stability and comfort. The Sure Horizon Retirement Income Strategy™ also takes a majority of the risks out of your retirement by taking advantage of the best characteristics of each of its components.

Throughout this chapter, we'll roll up our sleeves and dive into each segment. You'll learn not just the "what" and "how" but also the "why" behind each strategy. By the end, you'll have a personalized plan that isn't just a collection of numbers and charts but a clear, actionable path to a retirement that's as rewarding as it is secure.

Are you ready to take control of your retirement destiny? Let's get started, and remember, every step you take now is a step towards a better, more secure retirement. And don't worry. I'll guide you through each phase with practical tips and interactive exercises to help you apply what you learn directly to your unique situation. Let's build something great together!

Gathering Your Information

Welcome to the first crucial step in crafting your own Sure Horizon Retirement Income Strategy™! This chapter will use a hypothetical couple, Jack and Jill Smith, to illustrate how you will complete your plan. Just like Jack and Jill, as you begin by organizing all the necessary financial details that make up your life, you're not just doing busy work but laying the foundation upon which your entire retirement plan will be built. You're taking control of your financial future, and I'll guide you on how to do the same.

Jack and Jill's Example:

Jack and Jill started by listing their assets, income sources, and monthly expenses. They were thorough, ensuring everything was noticed because every piece of information can impact their retirement strategy.

- **Assets**: They included their 401(k) plans, Roth IRAs, and the current market value of their home.

  - Jack's 401(k): $575,000

  - Jill's 401(k): $235,000

  - Both have Roth IRAs valued at $50,000 each.

  - Their home was fully paid off and valued at $650,000.

- **Income Sources**:

- ◦ Jack's Pension: $1,000 per month

- ◦ Jack's Social Security: $2,850 per month (starting now at age 66)

- ◦ Jill's Social Security: $2,250 per month (starting at age 66, she is currently 64)

- **Monthly Essential Expenses**: Totaling $5,960, which covers all their necessities, including utilities, food, healthcare, and basic living costs.

- **Discretionary Spending Goals**: They plan to spend about $20,000 annually on travel and leisure activities, ensuring they enjoy their full retirement years.

Your Turn:

Now it's your turn to gather your financial details. Start by listing all your assets. These could include savings accounts, real estate, investment accounts, and any other significant assets. Next, outline all your expected income sources for retirement, such as pensions, social security, or any part-time work you plan to continue.

Lastly, as you calculate your monthly expenses, be reassured that you can constantly adjust these later as you refine your plan. If you're unsure about specific numbers, make an educated estimate for now. The important thing is to get started, and you can always make changes as you go.

We created a toolkit for you to use as you complete this exercise. Download the Retirement Income Toolkit from our companion website at www.SureHorizon-Retirement.com/Toolkit

Using the Retirement Income Toolkit: Access the toolkit on our website to input these figures. The toolkit is designed to guide you through each step, making it easy to see how each part of your financial picture contributes to your overall retirement strategy.

Gathering this information might take some time, but ensuring your retirement plan is robust, realistic, and tailored to your needs is critical. Remember, like Jack and Jill, you're setting the stage for a secure and fulfilling retirement. Let's make it count!

Now that you have this gathered, we will add the total investable portfolio assets to the Sure Horizon Retirement Income Strategy™ chart in your Retirement Income Toolkit, as the Smiths did below.

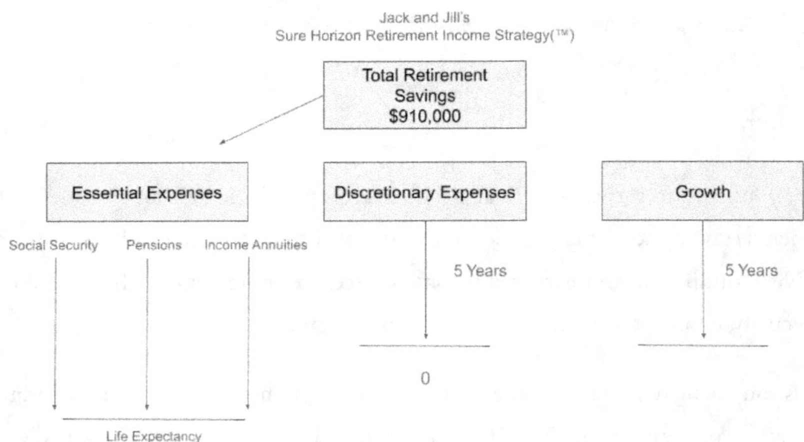

Building Your Essential Income Pool

Now that you've gathered all your financial information, it's time to structure the essential income component of your Sure Horizon Retirement Income Strategy™. This is where we ensure that stable, reliable income sources cover your essential monthly expenses. We'll use Jack and Jill as our guiding example to illustrate how they secured their essential income, and I'll help you do the same.

Jack and Jill's Strategy:

Jack and Jill began by adding up their guaranteed income sources:

- **Jack's Pension**: $1,000 per month

- **Jack's Social Security**: $2,850 per month

- **Jill's Social Security**: $2,250 per month (starting in two years)

Total monthly guaranteed income: $6,100

Next, they compared this total to their monthly essential expenses of $5,960. This left them with a small surplus each month. However, they wanted additional security to cover any unforeseen increases in living costs or unexpected expenses. They decided to purchase an immediate income annuity to bridge potential gaps and enhance their income security.

- **Immediate Annuity Purchase**: They used $180,000 from their savings to buy an annuity that pays $1,080 per month for life, ensuring they have more than enough to cover essentials and a bit extra for peace of mind.

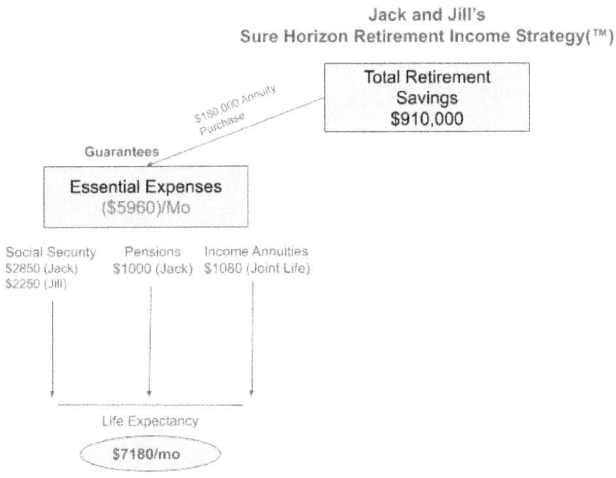

Your Turn:

Let's map out your essential income:

1. **Add Up Your Guaranteed Income Sources**:

○ Include all stable sources such as pensions, social security, or any other consistent income you expect to receive in retirement.

2. **Calculate Your Monthly Essential Expenses**:

○ Using the toolkit, enter the monthly essential expenses that you identified earlier.

3. **Identify Any Income Gaps**:

○ Subtract your total guaranteed income from your monthly expenses to see if there's a shortfall.

4. **Consider an Immediate Annuity** (if needed):

○ If you have a gap or want extra security, consider how much you need to invest in an immediate annuity to cover this difference. Use the annuity calculator in the toolkit to see how different amounts would affect your monthly income.

Using the Retirement Income Toolkit: Go to the Essential Income section of the toolkit and input this information.

Setting Up Your Discretionary Income Pool

Like Jack and Jill Smith, you can set up a bond ladder to manage your discretionary income needs during retirement. This approach allows you to enjoy the fruits of your labor without worrying about the market fluctuations impacting your annual vacation or hobby funds. Here's how to go about it:

Step 1: Determine Your Discretionary Income Needs

Start by defining how much you need each year for discretionary expenses. These could include travel, hobbies, dining out, gifts, and other non-essential but enjoyable activities. For example, Jack and Jill decided they needed $20,000 per year.

Step 2: Choose the Right Bonds for Your Ladder

Select bonds that mature each year to cover your annual discretionary spending. Depending on your tax situation and risk tolerance, this could be a mix of corporate, municipal, or treasury bonds. There are better places to take risks in your portfolio, so you want to select highly rated bonds that guarantee the money will be available each year that a bond matures. Aim to match the bond maturities with when you'll need the funds.

Step 3: Calculate the Initial Investment

Calculate how much money you need to invest to create your bond ladder. Each bond should be set to mature in a way that replenishes your fund annually. For example, if you need $20,000 per year, you may set up five bonds of $20,000 each, maturing one year apart.

Step 4: Implement and Monitor

Purchase the bonds and set up a schedule to monitor them annually. This type of portfolio is called a sinking fund, meaning it will slowly decline as each bond matures and is used. As each bond matures, the principal is used for your discretionary spending, and the interest earned can help offset inflation or be reinvested.

Step 5: Replenish as Necessary

Every five years, or as each bond matures, reassess your needs and the performance of your investments. You can reinvest in new bonds to continue the cycle, adjusting for any changes in your lifestyle or inflation.

By following these steps, you'll create a stable, predictable source of income for the fun parts of your retirement, much like Jack and Jill. Grab your Retirement Income Toolkit and plot your bond ladder on the provided template. This practical exercise will help you visualize and execute your plan efficiently.

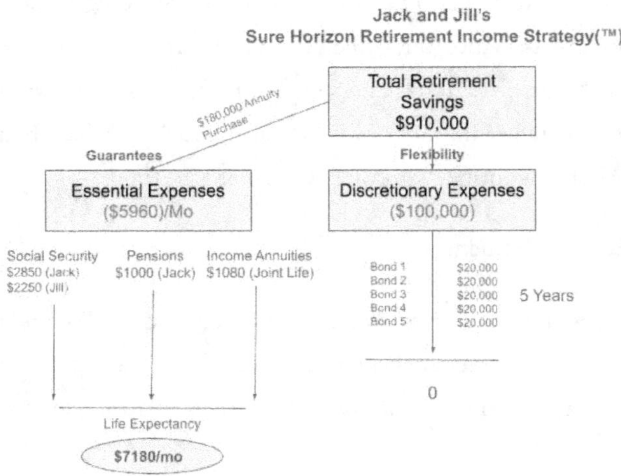

Calculating and Managing Your Growth Pool

Jack and Jill Smith's approach to managing their growth pool offers a practical example of ensuring long-term sustainability in funding retirement needs. Here's how you can apply similar steps to calculate and manage your growth pool effectively:

Step 1: Calculate the Initial Growth Pool

First, determine the total value of your current investment portfolio. From this total, subtract any amounts you have allocated to immediate needs, such as an income annuity or bond ladder. For Jack and Jill, this meant subtracting $180,000 from the annuity and $100,000 from the bond ladder from their retirement savings. Since the annuity will provide income for the rest of their lives, it will not need to be replenished in five years, so we would not use it as part of our Growth Pool.

Step 2: Set a Target for Growth

The next step is to decide how much money you need the growth pool to generate over a specific period, typically to replenish other segments of your plan, like the discretionary spending pool. Jack and Jill calculated the return needed on their growth pool to add $100,000 over five years, allowing them to replenish their bond ladder.

Step 3: Calculate the Required Rate of Return

To calculate your expected rate of return, you will need 3 pieces of data:

- Present Value (PV): The value where your portfolio is starting from

- Future Value (FV): The value where your portfolio will grow to

- Number of Periods (N): In this case, 5 years (or periods)

For those of you who are "mathy" the calculation for this is:

$$R = [\,(\,Ve - Vb\,)\, /\, Vb\,]\, x\, 100$$

Where,

R = Rate of return

Ve = End of period value

Vb = Beginning of period value

For those of you mere mortals in the audience (I don't do this without a calculator...I am one of you). You can go to the annual rate of return calculator created by our friends at Dinkytown.net (https://www.dinkytown.net/java/annual-rate-of-return-calculator.html)

Jack and Jill are starting with a portfolio (after removing the annuity purchase and discretionary pool) of $630,000 and aiming for their growth pool to grow by $100,000 over five years to $730,000. Their required rate of return, which you can see below in Figure 22.5, is 2.989%.

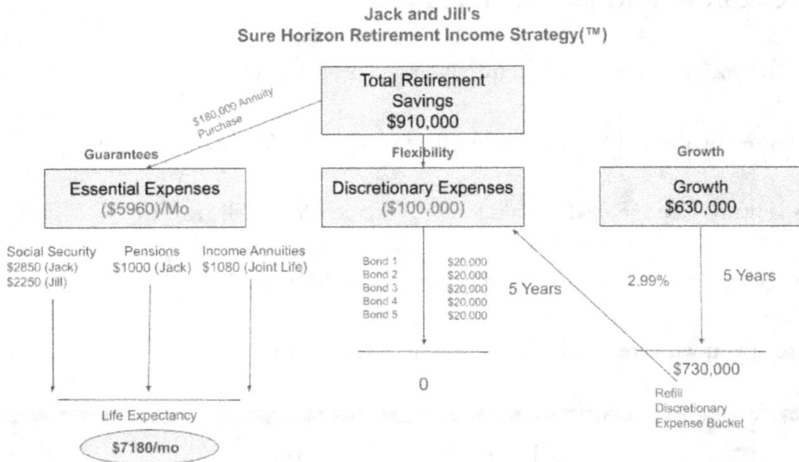

Sitting here in July of 2024, a money market fund is making around 5% (you wouldn't want to do that), so your chances of the plan working over the next five years are pretty good. This calculation determines how aggressively you need to be to achieve your goals.

If you would like to see me do this live, you can go to www.SureHorizonRetirement.com/Masterclass

Step 4: Invest According to Your Calculated Needs

Invest your growth pool in a diversified portfolio that matches the required rate of return while aligning with your risk tolerance. This might include a mix of stocks, bonds, mutual funds, and other investment vehicles that offer growth potential. Anything you make over your required rate of return pads your growth pool and helps if there is a market downturn in your future.

Step 5: Monitor and Adjust

Review the performance of your growth pool against your targets regularly. Adjust your strategy if your investments need to meet expectations or if economic conditions change. This may involve shifting asset allocations or investing in different financial instruments.

Step 6: Replenish and Repeat

Use the returns from your growth pool to replenish your discretionary fund or other income sources every five years or as planned. This step is crucial to maintaining a continuous flow of funds for your non-essential expenses without depleting your principal investment.

By following these steps, you'll maintain a dynamic and responsive approach to managing your retirement funds, ensuring that your immediate and future financial needs are met. Now, take some time to apply these calculations using the Retirement Income Toolkit. This exercise will help solidify your understanding and confidence in managing your retirement assets effectively.

Diversifying Your Growth Pool

Jack and Jill Smith's decision to diversify their growth pool illustrates a strategic approach to ensuring their investments are well-positioned for growth and risk management. Here's how you can follow their lead in diversifying your own growth pool:

Step 1: Decide on Your Asset Allocation

Just like Jack and Jill, begin by determining the composition of your growth pool. They chose a growth-oriented allocation involving:

- **60% U.S. Stocks**: Provides growth potential through equity exposure in the domestic market.

- **10% International Stocks**: Offers exposure to global markets, which can diversify risks and access growth opportunities outside the U.S.

- **10% Real Estate**: Adds a tangible asset class that offers rental income and price appreciation.

- **20% Diversified Bonds**: This category includes a mix of bond types, such as high-yield bonds, to provide income with a higher return potential than standard government or corporate bonds.

Step 2: Assess Your Risk Tolerance

Ensure that the chosen asset allocation aligns with your risk tolerance. A growth-oriented portfolio like Jack and Jill's aims for long-term growth but comes with higher volatility, particularly from the heavy stock and real estate components.

Step 3: Implement Your Investment Strategy

Invest in the chosen asset classes through various vehicles, such as mutual funds, ETFs, real estate investment trusts (REITs), and individual securities. Each vehicle has advantages and considerations, such as management fees, ease of liquidity, and tax implications.

Step 4: Rebalance Regularly

Market movements can cause your initial asset allocation to drift over time. Regular rebalancing—returning your portfolio to its target allocations—helps maintain your desired risk level and investment strategy. This might mean selling some assets that have grown beyond their target percentage and buying more of others that have underperformed.

Step 5: Monitor and Adjust as Needed

Keep an eye on how each segment of your portfolio performs and how global economic changes might impact your investments. This ongoing monitoring will inform whether you need to adjust your strategy to respond to changes in the market or in your own financial goals.

Exercise: Now, using the Retirement Income Toolkit, plot out a diversified growth portfolio based on your retirement goals and risk tolerance. Experiment with different allocations and see how changes affect potential returns and risks. This practical exercise will help you understand the dynamics of a diversified portfolio and how to adjust it to meet your evolving needs.

By diversifying your growth pool, you will enhance your ability to cope with market fluctuations and improve your prospects for robust long-term growth. This approach supports your immediate retirement needs and secures your financial future against many potential scenarios.

Integrating Long-Term Care Coverage into the Retirement Plan

After carefully reviewing their overall retirement plan, Jack and Jill Smith decided to further reduce their financial risks by investing in an asset-based long-term care policy. Here's how they approached this decision and how you can consider a similar strategy:

Step 1: Evaluate the Need for Long-Term Care Coverage

Recognizing the potential need for long-term care and its significant costs, Jack and Jill proactively managed this risk. They opted for an asset-based long-term care policy, which provides care coverage and benefits their heirs if the coverage is not utilized.

Step 2: Understanding Asset-Based Long-Term Care Policies

Asset-based long-term care policies combine life insurance with long-term care coverage. These policies allow you to:

- **Use the benefits for long-term care**: If Jack or Jill requires long-term care, the policy provides a daily benefit of $200 to cover those costs.

- **Leave a death benefit**: If they do not use the long-term care benefits, a death benefit of $232,000 will be paid to their estate after both pass away. This feature ensures that their investment in the policy is not lost but can benefit their family.

Step 3: Financial Considerations and Policy Purchase

Jack and Jill invested $100,000 into the policy, considering it a part of their diversified retirement strategy. With the particular policy they bought, they could leverage their long-term care to be a total of $400,000 coverage when needed. Additionally, all the money from the policy will be tax-free if used for long-term care. This amount secures the long-term care coverage they might need while preserving the value of their estate.

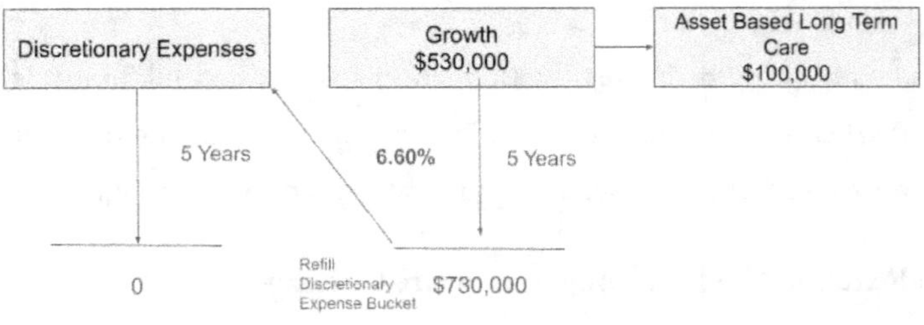

Step 4: Going Through Underwriting

To qualify for the policy, they underwent an underwriting process that assessed their health and other risk factors. Qualifying for this type of insurance typically involves a review of medical history and current health status, underlining the importance of considering such insurance while still in good health.

Step 5: Integrating the Policy into Their Financial Plan

By choosing an asset-based policy, they effectively created a fallback option that addresses potential long-term care needs and estate planning goals. This strategic move helps them feel secure, knowing they have prepared for multiple outcomes.

Exercise: Using the Retirement Income Toolkit, analyze how an asset-based or long-term care policy might fit into your retirement strategy. Consider your health, potential long-term care needs, and estate planning goals. Calculate how reallocating funds into such a policy could impact your retirement security and estate value.

Jack and Jill's decision to integrate long-term care insurance into their retirement planning provides peace of mind and financial security, ensuring they are well-prepared for the uncertainties of aging. Similarly, assessing your need for such coverage and understanding the dual benefits of asset-based policies can be crucial steps in crafting a comprehensive retirement plan.

Implementing a "Lifeboat Strategy" with a Reverse Mortgage

As a final layer of financial protection, Jack and Jill Smith considered how they could safeguard their retirement income against market volatility. Their solution involved strategically using a reverse mortgage as a standby resource. Here's how they implemented this approach:

Step 1: Evaluating Their Home Equity

Jack and Jill consulted with a reverse mortgage specialist to assess the potential of tapping into their home's equity, valued at $650,000. They learned they could secure approximately $275,000 through a reverse mortgage, giving them a substantial reserve without the obligation to make monthly payments.

Step 2: Understanding the Reverse Mortgage

A reverse mortgage allows homeowners aged 62 and older to convert part of the equity in their home into cash. This product's beauty lies in its flexibility—the funds are available when needed but do not require immediate repayment as long as the homeowners live in the home and meet the mortgage terms.

Step 3: Designing the "Lifeboat Strategy"

Jack and Jill used the reverse mortgage as a financial "lifeboat." This strategy allowed them to draw on the reverse mortgage funds during market downturns, precisely if they needed to replenish their Discretionary Bond Ladder while their Growth Pool was underperforming. This approach effectively mitigates the sequence of returns risk, where withdrawing funds during a market downturn can significantly impact the longevity of a retiree's portfolio. The cost of setting up this plan is 2% of the loan amount, in this case $275,000. This amount was rolled into the loan at the closing.

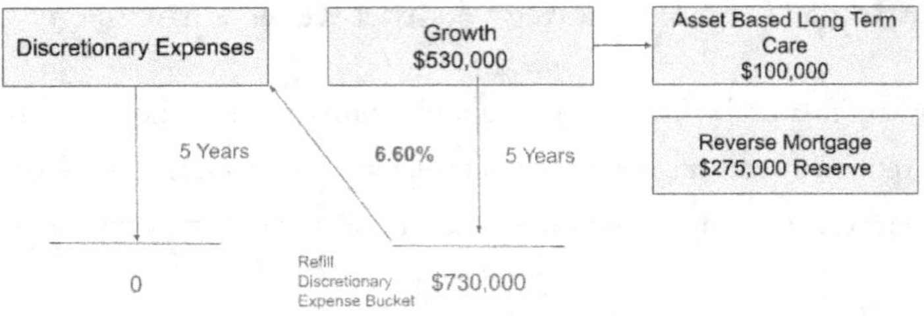

Step 4: Implementing the Strategy

They set up the reverse mortgage but waited to draw on it. Instead, they kept it as a ready reserve. This setup ensures that if the market is down when it's time to re-fund their Discretionary Bond Ladder, they can use the reverse mortgage funds instead of selling investments at a loss.

Step 5: Planning for Market Recovery

Their strategy includes the option to repay the reverse mortgage funds if the market recovers and their investments bounce back. This flexibility allows them to manage their assets more effectively and maintain the value of their home equity as part of their estate.

Exercise: Using the Retirement Income Toolkit, simulate how a reverse mortgage could be a financial safety net for your retirement plan. Calculate how having access to home equity might impact your decisions during various market conditions, especially when considering withdrawals from investment accounts.

Jack and Jill have enhanced their financial security by incorporating a reverse mortgage into their retirement income plan. They appreciate the peace of mind of knowing they have a buffer against market volatility, preserving their investment accounts during downturns, and providing more stability for their financial future. This strategic use of home equity protects their assets and ensures they can maintain their lifestyle without compromise.

Wrapping Up Your Sure Horizon Retirement Income Strategy™

As we conclude this chapter on building your Sure Horizon Retirement Income Strategy™, let's recap the essential steps we've walked through using Jack and Jill Smith as our guiding example. Their journey through planning highlights the critical importance of having a structured yet flexible approach to retirement.

Critical Steps in Building Your Retirement Income Plan:

1. **Gather Your Data**: Just as Jack and Jill did, start by collecting all relevant financial information. This includes your savings, investments, expected Social Security benefits, and other income sources. Use the Retirement Income Toolkit to organize and visualize this data.

2. **Plan for Essential Income**: Identify your essential monthly expenses and match them with guaranteed income sources like Social Security, pensions, or annuities. This step ensures that your basic needs are always covered, giving you peace of mind.

3. **Manage Discretionary Spending**: Decide how much you'd like to spend on the enjoyable aspects of retirement, such as travel and hobbies. Jack and Jill used a bond ladder to manage these expenses, ensuring they had fun money without dipping into essential funds.

4. **Secure Growth for the Future**: Calculate the size and expected return of your Growth Pool. This is where your portfolio works to combat inflation and grow wealth over time. Remember, this fund is critical for replenishing your Discretionary Fund and covering unexpected long-term costs.

5. **Incorporate Safeguards**: Consider strategies like long-term care insurance or a reverse mortgage as part of your plan to protect against unexpected financial strains. These tools can provide substantial security when facing healthcare needs or market downturns.

6. **Regular Reviews and Adjustments**: Make it a habit to review your plan annually or whenever significant life changes occur. This adaptability is crucial for responding effectively to new circumstances and market conditions.

Final Encouragement and Call to Action:

Now that you've seen how to construct a comprehensive retirement income plan, it's your turn to implement these strategies. Use the tools and exercises in the Retirement Income Toolkit to start crafting a plan tailored to your unique needs and goals. Remember, the journey to a secure and fulfilling retirement is ongoing, and starting your planning today puts you in control of your financial future.

Don't hesitate to revisit your plan regularly and make adjustments as needed. Life's unpredictable nature means flexibility isn't just beneficial—it's essential. By staying proactive and engaged with your retirement planning, you can ensure that your golden years are as rewarding and secure as you aspire.

Start today by downloading the Retirement Income Toolkit and taking the first steps toward building your Sure Horizon Retirement Income Strategy™. It's never too early or too late to begin shaping your retirement dreams into reality.

Chapter 23

Conclusion: Your Path to a Secure and Rewarding Retirement

"Your retirement is your time to thrive—prepare wisely, plan thoroughly, and live fully."

As we conclude our comprehensive exploration of retirement planning, it's crucial to reflect on the essential strategies and concepts we've covered. This book has been a journey through the detailed facets of creating a stable and fulfilling retirement, using the Sure Horizon Retirement Income Strategy™ as our guide. This strategy ensures that your essential expenses are covered with guaranteed income, your lifestyle is enriched through flexible discretionary income, and your future is secured with growth-oriented investments.

Embrace the Journey

Retirement planning is more than just a financial task; it's a profound commitment to your future self. It requires foresight, discipline, and an understanding that while the road may shift, your control over your financial destiny is paramount. By following the structured approach of the 3 x 3 Retirement Income Strategy™, you're not just preparing financially—you're ensuring that your retirement years are as vibrant and secure as possible, giving you a sense of control and empowerment over your future.

Learn from Real-Life Applications

Consider the story of Jack and Jill Smith, which we shared with you in the last chapter. They could have started with a better plan. Still, through careful consideration, using tools like the Retirement Income Toolkit, and adapting to their evolving needs, they crafted a strategy that promises them security and enjoyment in their retirement years. Let their story inspire you to take action and believe in the power of well-informed, proactive planning, instilling a sense of motivation and hope in your own retirement planning journey.

Tools at Your Disposal

You can access a wealth of resources to facilitate your planning process. Your starting point is the "Retirement Income Toolkit," available at www.SureHorizonRetirement.com/Toolkit. This toolkit includes calculators, templates, and guides that simplify complex calculations and scenarios, making it easier to understand and apply the principles discussed in each chapter.

The Importance of Adaptability

Retirement planning is not a static process. Just as life evolves, so should your retirement plan. Economic conditions change, personal circumstances shift, and new financial products become available. Staying informed and flexible allows you to adjust your strategy to maximize financial security and personal happiness.

Continuous Learning and Community Engagement

Engage with online and offline communities focusing on retirement planning and financial literacy. Participate in workshops, seminars, and webinars to stay updated on the latest trends and strategies. The more you learn, the better equipped you'll be to make informed decisions that enhance your retirement readiness. The more you engage with these communities, the more supported and part of a larger network you'll feel.

Professional Guidance

While this book provides a comprehensive guide to retirement planning, personalized advice from financial professionals is invaluable. A financial advisor can offer customized insights and strategies tailored to your unique financial situation, helping you confidently navigate complex decisions.

Your Call to Action

Don't wait for the perfect moment to start planning your retirement. The best time to start is now. Whether reassessing your current financial plan, scheduling a consultation with a financial advisor, or simply educating yourself about your options, every step you take is progress.

Lifelong Journey

Approach retirement planning as a lifelong journey, not a destination. Regular reviews and adjustments of your plan are crucial as you transition through different phases of life. Each review is an opportunity to optimize your strategies and ensure your retirement goals are on track.

The Power of a Positive Outlook

Maintain a positive outlook throughout your planning process. Believe in creating a financially secure and rich retirement experience and opportunity. Use the tools and strategies you've learned to build a retirement you look forward to, one that truly reflects your aspirations and dreams.

Conclusion

As you turn the final page of this book, remember that the chapters here are just the beginning of your active engagement with your retirement future. The strategies, advice, and tools provided are designed to empower you to take control, make informed decisions, and enter your retirement years with confidence and clarity. Your efforts now will define the quality of your life in retirement. Make it a priority, make it successful, and most importantly, make it yours.

Armed with knowledge, resources, and a proactive mindset, you're ready to navigate the challenges and seize the opportunities that come with planning for retirement. Let's make these years your best yet. It's time to take that first step into a future you've not only imagined but have meticulously planned for. Here's to a fulfilling and secure retirement!

Glossary of Terms

3 x 3 Retirement Income Strategy™: A holistic retirement planning framework developed by Jeff Kikel, this strategy integrates three fundamental goals—guarantees, Flexibility, and Growth—into three pools: Essential, Discretionary, and Growth pools, to provide a balanced approach to retirement income planning.

Annuities: Financial products offered by insurance companies that guarantee to pay a fixed stream of income to the annuitant for a specified term or life, often used as part of retirement planning to provide predictable income.

Asset Allocation: The process of dividing investments among different asset categories, such as stocks, bonds, and real estate, to optimize the balance between risk and reward based on individual retirement goals and risk tolerance.

Bond Ladder: An investment strategy where bonds with different maturities are arranged in a ladder structure. As each bond matures, the principal is reinvested in new bonds at the long end of the ladder, helping to manage interest rate risk and provide consistent income.

Discretionary Income Pool: This part of the retirement income plan includes income for non-essential expenditures that enhance lifestyle and enjoyment, such as travel, hobbies, and luxury items.

Diversified Portfolio: An investment strategy that involves spreading assets among various types of investments (stocks, bonds, real estate, etc.) to reduce exposure to any single asset class and mitigate risk.

Essential Income Pool: The part of a retirement income strategy that ensures all basic and non-negotiable living expenses are met. This pool typically includes income from guaranteed sources like Social Security, pensions, or certain annuities.

Fixed Income Strategy: An approach that primarily relies on investments like bonds or bond funds, which provide regular income payouts. These investments are generally considered lower risk compared to equities.

Flexibility: The capability of an investment or financial plan to adapt to life changes and unexpected financial demands without significant sacrifices or risks.

Growth: The objective of ensuring that investments increase in value over time, typically through equities or other assets that offer the potential for capital appreciation.

Guarantees: Financial strategies or products that offer assured income or returns, typically involving less risk and providing a stable income stream, such as fixed annuities or government bonds.

Income Annuities: An annuity contract that converts part of the holder's savings into periodic payments that can last for life or a specified period. Useful for managing longevity risk.

Inflation Risk: The danger that inflation will undermine the real purchasing power of assets or income is particularly significant for retirees who may be on fixed incomes.

Longevity Risk: The risk of outliving one's retirement savings. This is a critical factor in retirement planning, influencing decisions on pensions, annuities, and withdrawal rates.

Market Volatility: he rate at which the price of investments increases or decreases for a given set of returns. Planning for volatility is crucial in retirement planning to ensure that income streams are not adversely affected.

Pensions: Retirement plans that provide a fixed, regular payment from an employer to an employee, typically after retirement. The amount often depends on the employee's salary history and tenure of service.

Social Security: A federal program in the United States that provides retirement income for elderly citizens or disabled individuals. Benefits are calculated based on a person's previous earnings and are adjusted for inflation.

Strategic Planning: The process of setting goals, assessing the current financial situation, and creating an action plan that aligns with one's retirement objectives and available resources.

Index

A

- **Flexibility in Retirement Planning**

  - Adapting to change, 53, 155, 185

  - Managing discretionary income, 143, 169

  - Importance in long-term planning, 53, 185

G

- **Guaranteed Income**

  - Overview and significance, 41, 123

  - Sources (Social Security, Pensions, Annuities), 41, 97, 111

  - Case studies, 251, 273, 317

  - Stability and predictability, 41, 123, 251

- **Growth Pool**

  - Role in beating inflation, 199

  - Investment strategies, 199, 237

  - Replenishing the Discretionary Pool, 237

  - Long-term growth strategies, 199, 237

H

- **Healthcare Costs**

  - Planning for healthcare in retirement, 9, 97, 273

  - Long-term care needs, 273, 305

  - Impact on retirement planning, 9, 273, 305

I

About The Author

 Jeff Kikel brings over three decades of experience in financial services, specializing in Retirement Income Planning and Financial Planning. A distinguished author, Jeff has written nine influential books before publishing "The Retirement Income Equation." He holds a BA in Personal Financial Planning from Texas Tech University and maintains several prestigious designations, including Chartered Financial Consultant (ChFC), Chartered Retirement Planning Counselor (CRPC), Certified College Funding Specialist (CCFS), and Accredited Small Business Consultant (ASBC).

As a Registered Investment Advisor and Licensed Insurance Agent, Jeff has dedicated his career to helping individuals navigate the complexities of retirement planning. His deep commitment to financial education is evident in his forthcoming book, "Overcoming the Retirement Trap," aimed at aiding Late Gen X and Early Millennials in achieving financial freedom, time freedom, and freedom of intentionality.

When he's not demystifying financial concepts for his readers or clients, Jeff enjoys traveling the world, writing, and spending quality time with his wife and business partner, Crystal. Together, they continue exploring new strategies to empower others to plan a secure and prosperous retirement.

Books By Jeff Kikel

The Sure Horizon Retirement Series

- *The Retirement Income Equation: Proven Strategies for Secure, Flexible, and Prosperous Retirement*

- *7 Critical Mistakes To Avoid In Retirement Planning: A Comprehensive Guide to Avoiding Common Pitfalls and Securing Your Financial Future*

Freedom Day Series

- *Overcoming the Retirement Trap: An 8-Step Financial Freedom Blueprint For Your Journey To Building Wealth, Creating Financial Independence, And A Life Beyond Limits*

Family Playbook Series

- *The Family Financial Playbook: Essential Strategies For Building Financial Literacy Together* **(#1 New Release in Budgeting on Amazon)**

- *The Family Investment Playbook: Essential Strategies for Building An Investment Portfolio As A Family*

NexGen CEO Series

- *The Young Entrepreneurs Starter Kit: An Essential Guide For Teens To Learn Business Skills, Create A Business, And Generate Extra Income*

- *The Parents Guide To Raising Business Smart Kids*

With Joe Serio, PhD

- *Leaving Blue: 50 Lessons On Retiring Well From Law Enforcement*

With Gary Kasper

- *Identity Theft: The Road To Recovery*

Keep the Wisdom Flowing

Now that you've equipped yourself with the strategies and insights from *The Retirement Income Equation*, it's time to pass on the torch of knowledge. Your journey towards a secure, flexible, and prosperous retirement is well underway, and you can help others embark on theirs.

By sharing your honest review of this book on Amazon, you're not just recommending a book—you're guiding future retirees toward a path of financial wisdom and empowerment. Your thoughts and feedback are not just valuable, but they can significantly influence someone else's retirement planning, steering them toward making informed and effective decisions. Your review could be the key that unlocks a secure and prosperous retirement for someone else.

Thank you for your invaluable contribution. The legacy of well-planned retirements grows stronger with each shared experience and every piece of advice passed forward. Together, we're building a community of savvy retirees ready to embrace their golden years with confidence and joy.

Please take a moment to leave your review here:

https://www.amazon.com/review/review-your-purchases/?asin=B0DCLRV2ST

Your unique insights ensure that the wisdom of *The Retirement Income Equation* continues to inspire and assist others just like you. You are a crucial part of this journey, and your continued involvement is key to our collective success. Thank you for being a part of this community.

Jeff Kikel

Your Stress-Free Retirement Guide